GLAD NEWS!

GLAD NEWS!

God Loves You, My Muslim Friend

SAMY TANAGHO

MOODY PUBLISHERS

CHICAGO

2017 edition edited by Linda Joy Neufeld
Interior design: Ragont Design
Cover design: Erik M. Peterson
Cover photo of daisies copyright (c) 2009 by afhunta/iStock (91742264). All rights reserved.

Library of Congress Cataloging-in-Publication Data

Names: Tanagho, Samy, author.
Title: Glad news! God loves you, my Muslim friend / by Samy Tanagho.
Description: Chicago : Moody Publishers, 2017. | Previously published:
  Colorado Springs : Authentic Media, 2004. | Includes bibliographical
  references.
Identifiers: LCCN 2016059268 | ISBN 9780802416582
Subjects: LCSH: Missions to Muslims. | Islam--Relations--Christianity. |
  Christianity and other religions--Islam.
Classification: LCC BV2625 .T36 2017 | DDC 266.0088/297--dc23
LC record available at https://lccn.loc.gov/2016059268

We hope you enjoy this book from Moody Publishers. Our goal is to provide high-quality, thought-provoking books and products that connect truth to your real needs and challenges. For more information on other books and products written and produced from a biblical perspective, go to www.moodypublishers.com or write to:

Moody Publishers
820 N. LaSalle Boulevard
Chicago, IL 60610

1 3 5 7 9 10 8 6 4 2

Printed in the United States of America

**Assalam Alaikum,
my precious Muslim friends.**

God promised Abraham: "And as for Ishmael, I have
heard you: I will surely bless him; I will make him fruitful
and will greatly increase his numbers." (GENESIS 17:20)

I dedicate this book to my precious Muslim acquaintances,
friends, neighbors, and all the sincere Muslims in the world who
are earnestly seeking to have a complete relationship with the
Living God (*Allah AL-Hayy*, in Arabic).

My dear reader, I believe God orchestrated many events to
get this book in your hands to have you read it.

God knows you. You matter to Him. Because He loves you,
He wants to give you the best life possible here on earth. He
wants you to live with Him forever and enjoy His kingdom, His
presence, and His love. This is His purpose for creating you.

This is His joy, to love you and see you happy.

Glad News!
God loves you, my Muslim friend.

God loves you so much and He wants to embrace you as a father embraces his child. Yes, God wants you to become His child. He wants to have a close relationship with you based not on fear but on mutual love! God created you to enjoy joyful, unbroken fellowship with Him forever.

God does not desire our relationship with Him to consist only of religious rituals and traditions. There is something deeper God desires for each one of us to have. God wants you to know Him through a living relationship and experience His love, forgiveness, and divine presence. The invitation is open to you.

God is inviting you to enjoy His salvation and discover the depth of His love toward you.

Understanding and applying God's truth is available for all humanity—God has given us the ability to become spiritually enlightened and alive! God desires to fill your life with joy, love, peace, and hope.

God designed us in such a way that we will never be completely satisfied and happy without experiencing His perfect will in our lives. The way to enjoy the right relationship with God is presented to you in this book.

> "You will seek me and find me when you seek
> me with all your heart." (JEREMIAH 29:13)

CONTENTS

SECTION NINE
The Myth of the Three Gods of Christianity

SECTION TEN
Worship, Love, and the Savior

INTRODUCTION

Everyone searches for love, but for many it proves elusive. The Beatles sang "All You Need Is Love" and then they disbanded! Many couples think they have found love, but then it slips away from them. They wonder if it was true love after all. I want to tell you about *real love*, an unconditional love that will revolutionize your life. In fact, it is the greatest love story in human history—God's love for *you*!

The most prevalent characteristic revealed about God in the Bible is that He is a loving God. Love is not just one of God's glorious attributes; love is the essence of God's being.

THE GOD OF LOVE

Since February 1976, I have been experiencing God's deep love. I have met thousands of true followers of Christ who have had and still have the same experience. It is stated in the Bible, "We know and rely on the love God has for us. God is love" (1 John 4:16).

The God of the Bible does not merely love you, and me, and

all people . . . "God is love." This is the message I want to share with you. My desire is that multitudes of Muslims will know and experience God's deep and personal love for them. This longing has prompted me to write to you. I grew up with Muslim school-mates and neighbors, eating, studying, playing soccer, and swim-ming with them. Throughout my life, many of my best friends were Muslims. My wife was born and raised as a Muslim. I love Muslims. By the way, all true followers of Jesus Christ should deeply and genuinely love all Muslims.

The Qur'an states, "Strongest among men in enmity to the believers [Muslims] wilt thou find the Jews and Pagans; and nearest among them in love to the believers wilt thou find those who say 'we are Christians': because amongst these are men de-voted to learning and men who have renounced the world, and they are not arrogant" (Surah 5:82).

In fact, Muhammad himself relied on Christians when Mus-lims were being persecuted. Islamic historians and books record that Muhammad trusted his Christian friends in Abyssinia and sent his followers there to be protected by followers of Jesus Christ.[1]

The Qur'an mentions the glad news of Jesus in Surah 3:45 "Behold! The angel said: 'O Mary! Allah giveth thee Glad Tidings of a Word from him: His name will be Christ Jesus . . .'"

Jesus Christ is the most important person in the Bible, and the Qur'an refers to Jesus Christ (called *AL-Masih Isa* in the Qur'an) about ninety times, where Muhammad is mentioned only a few times. This book examines what the Bible and the Qur'an say about Jesus. It is very important that you read this book, so you can discover who Jesus Christ really is.

We read in the Qur'an: "Behold! Allah said: 'O Jesus . . . I will make those who follow you superior to those who reject faith, to the Day of Resurrection'" (Surah 3:55).

My prayer is that you will have an open mind and sincerity

in your search for the truth. I also pray that you will ask God to guide you before, during, and after reading this book.

THE HEART OF GOD

My dear Muslim friend, God is speaking to me and to you:

"I know the plans I have for you," declares the LORD, "plans to prosper you and not to harm you, plans to give you hope and a future." (Jeremiah 29:11)

Please consider the heart of God toward you. The following passage gives a glimpse of God's love for you and for all those who are not secure in His arms.

Jesus taught this parable:

What do you think? If a man owns a hundred sheep, and one of them wanders away, will he not leave the ninety-nine [secure sheep] on the hills and go to look for the one that wandered off? And if he finds it, I truly tell you, he is happier about that one [lost] sheep than about the ninety-nine that did not wander off. In the same way your Father in heaven is not willing that any of these little ones should perish. (Matthew 18:12–14)

Jesus wants us to know that God relentlessly pursues us at any time when we are lost.

My precious reader, it is not by accident you are reading this book right now. It is a divine appointment designed by the relational God to draw you to know Him because God is passionate in His love toward you.

You owe it to yourself and to God to investigate and see if what the Bible says is true.

SAMY TANAGHO

SECTION ONE

THE QUR'AN'S TESTIMONY REGARDING THE AUTHENTICITY OF THE BIBLE

1

THE CREDIBILITY
OF THE BIBLE

In this book, Islamic beliefs and verses from the Qur'an are discussed to help Muslims and Christians see the common ground and the differences between Islam and Christianity.

While I do not depend on the Qur'an to prove the credibility of the Bible, I find it significant and interesting that throughout its pages, the Qur'an testifies to the authenticity of the Bible. The Jews and the Christians are described in the Qur'an as "the people of the Book." The Jewish Scripture is the Torah; and the Christian Scripture is the Injeel. The Qur'an speaks with reverence and respect of the Torah (Old Testament), Zabur (the Psalms), and the Injeel (Gospel or New Testament). These Holy Scriptures, according to the Qur'an, have the status of the authentic Word of God, because they were God's revelation before the Qur'an.

The Torah can mean the "law" or the instruction God gave through Moses. Also, it can be any word God gave through the prophets.

My dear Muslim friend, there is not one single verse in the Qur'an that confirms that the Bible has been invalidated by the arrival of the Qur'an. Furthermore, the Qur'an itself commands Muslims to profess belief in the Bible. We read in Surah 2:136: "Say ye: 'We believe in Allah, and the revelation given to us, and to Abraham . . . and that given to Moses and Jesus, and that given to [all] Prophets from their Lord: We make no difference between one and another of them . . .'"

THE QUR'AN CONFIRMS HOLY SCRIPTURE

Hundreds of years before the time of Muhammad, the Bible was already written and in the hands of people all over the world. The Qur'an declares that it (the Qur'an) was given to confirm the previous revelations and not to replace them. Surah 5:48 says: "To thee [Muhammad] We sent the Scripture [Qur'an] in truth confirming the Scripture that came before it; and guarding it in safety." This confirmation is repeated in many Qur'anic verses (Surah 2:89; 2:91, 97; 2:101; 6:92; 46:12).

The Qur'an testifies that the Torah, the Zabur, and the Injeel are the Word of God. The testimony of the Qur'an is clear. Surah 3:3–4 states: "And He [God] sent down the Law [of Moses] and the gospel (of Jesus) before this as a guide to mankind."

The Qur'an's References to the Torah

Regarding the Torah, we read in Surah 5:44: "It was We who revealed the Law (to Moses) therein was guidance and light. By its standard have been judged the Jews, by the prophets who bowed (as in Islam) to Allah's will." Other verses in the Qur'an that discuss the Torah are as follows:

"We gave Moses the Book, completing (Our favor) to those who would do right, and explaining all things in detail—and a guide and a mercy." (Surah 6:154)

"We [God] gave Moses the Book and followed him up with a succession of Messengers [Jewish prophets]." (Surah 2:87) Please refer also to Surah 4:54; 28:43; 32:23; 40:53–54; and 45:16.

The Qur'an's References to the Zabur (Psalms) and Injeel

Regarding the Zabur, the Qur'an states in Surah 21:105, "Before this We [God] wrote in the Psalms . . ."

Regarding the Injeel, the Qur'an declares in Surah 5:46, "And in their footsteps We sent Jesus the son of Mary, confirming the law that had come before him: We sent him the gospel: therein was guidance and light and confirmation of the law that had come before him: a guidance and an admonition to those who fear Allah." Please also read Surah 57:27.

ACCORDING TO THE QUR'AN ALL HOLY BOOKS ARE EQUAL

Many Muslims think that it is unnecessary to read the Bible. Their opinion contradicts even the Qur'an itself. The Qur'an states clearly that all Muslims must follow and obey the teachings of the previous Holy Scripture (the Bible). The following Surahs are clear on this subject:

Surah 2:285 states: "The Messenger believeth in what hath been revealed to him from his Lord, as do the men of faith. Each one (of them) believeth in Allah, His angels, His books, and His Messengers. 'We make no distinction (they say) between one and another of His Messengers.' And they say: 'We hear and we obey . . .'"

Surah 4:136 reads: "O ye who believe! Believe in Allah and His Messenger and the scripture which He hath sent to His Messenger and the scripture which He sent to those before (him). Any who denieth Allah, His angels, His Books, His Messengers, and the Day of Judgment hath gone far, far astray."

In Surah 2:285 and Surah 4:136 cited above, notice that "His Books" is plural. This means all the Holy Books. This is a clear command that Muslims should regard all Holy Books as equal revelation.

As we read in Surah 4:136, if any Muslim ignores or rejects any part of God's revelation in the Torah or in the Gospel, he has "gone far, far astray." Also, God would condemn him as an infidel, as noted in Surah 40:70–72: "Those who reject the Book and the (revelations) with which We sent Our messengers: But soon shall they know—when the yokes (shall be) round their necks, and the chains; They shall be dragged along—In the boiling fetid fluid; Then in the Fire shall They be burned."

Clearly, the Qur'an commands all people to read and obey God's revelations in the Bible; this is an essential part of being a Muslim. It is very clear that Muhammad himself considered the Holy Scriptures of the Jews and the Christians to be books that lead people to become fully submitted to God.

The Qur'an also indicates that the Jews and Christians who lived in Muhammad's time rejected the Qur'an. You can read about this in Surah 2:91: "When it is said to them: 'Believe in what Allah hath sent down,' they say, 'We believe in what was sent down to us.' Yet they reject all besides, even if it be truth confirming what is with them."

It is a fact that Muhammad wanted Arab Christians and Jews to accept him as a prophet in the line of biblical prophets. The Qur'an also recorded that Jews and Christians rejected Muhammad (Surah 2:120).

The Qur'an Considers the Bible Preeminent

Surah 10:94 is a command given to Muhammad (and all Muslims) to treat the Bible as the primary source of enlightenment: "If thou [Muhammad] wert in doubt as to what We have revealed unto thee then ask those who have been reading the Book from before thee." This verse clearly instructs all the Muslim believers to refer to the Bible when questions arise regarding the Qur'an's meaning. It is clear from this verse that in the event of any doubt about certain revelations in the Qur'an, Muhammad is commanded by God to consult with the Jews and Christians who have been reading their Holy Scriptures. So Surah 10:94 is a command to Muhammad to test the truthfulness of his own message by the contents of the Holy Scriptures of the Jews and the Christians. This verse clearly shows that the Qur'an does not supersede the Gospel.

If Muhammad had doubt and was commanded to ask, then you, as a Muslim, have the permission–and the obligation–to examine all things. Think about all the information you receive so you can, by God's guidance, determine the whole truth.

My dear friend, the Qur'an does not claim that God sent it to prevent corruption or to replace the Holy Word of God, which is the entire Bible (Torah and the Injeel). On the contrary, the Qur'an confirms biblical authenticity.

Jesus declared that He did not come to abrogate previous revelations. Jesus said, "Do not think that I have come to abolish the Law or the Prophets; I have not come to abolish them but to fulfill them" (Matthew 5:17).

The Qur'an Recognizes That the Jews Possess the Word of God

For example, a dispute had arisen among the Jews in Medina, and it had come to the attention of Muhammad. The Qur'an addresses Muhammad, "But why do they come to thee for decision, when they have [their own] law before them? Therein is the [plain] command of Allah" (Surah 5:43). Notice the expression "before them" in this verse.

It is also clear from Surah 5:43 that it was not necessary for the Jews to go to Muhammad for judgment because they had their Holy Scripture, which is the Word of God that contained all the needed guidance and light.

Consider also Surah 2:101, which states, "And when there came to them a Messenger from Allah, confirming what was with them." Notice the expression "with them." These verses clearly teach that the Jews of Medina had the Old Testament in their possession at the time of Muhammad, and it was reliable to settle their own disputes.

Throughout their history, the Jews have known only the Holy Scripture in the Books of the Old Testament. The Qur'an never states that the Torah is a book different from that which the Jews themselves accepted as the Torah.

The Qur'an Recognizes That the Christians Possess the Word of God

The Qur'an also confirms biblical authenticity with regard to the New Testament. Surah 5:47 states, "Let the people of the gospel judge by what Allah hath revealed therein. If any do fail to judge by (the light of) what Allah hath revealed, they are (no better than) those who rebel." How could the Christians be expected to judge by the Injeel unless they had it in their possession? The Christian world has known only one Injeel, which existed centuries before Muhammad's time and continues to exist today. The Qur'an never states that the Gospel is a book different from the one Christians used at the time of Muhammad. And the Qur'an never accuses the Jews and Christians of changing the actual text of the biblical manuscripts.

Have you noticed, my precious Muslim reader, what this verse said? "Let the people of the gospel judge by what Allah hath revealed therein." So the Christians, who are the people of the Gospel, should rely on the Gospel. They do not need the Qur'an.

It is clear then—the Qur'an does not supersede the Gospel!

The Qur'an in Surah 5:47 uses the word *Injeel*, which is the same title that the followers of Jesus use. Please refer to Mark 1:1 (NKJV): "The beginning of the gospel of Jesus Christ . . ." In fact, Christian Arabs still use the Arabic word *Injeel* for the Gospel.

Additional References to the Torah and the Gospel

It is important to note that the Qur'an does not claim to give all the teachings of Jesus, nor the whole story of His life. You need to read the New Testament to discover all that Jesus taught.

The Qur'an confirms its support of the Torah and the Gospel and urges the Jews and the Christians to recognize the authority of their Holy Book. It says in Surah 5:68, "Say: 'O People of the Book! Ye have no ground to stand upon unless ye stand fast by the Law, the gospel, and all the revelation that has come to you from your Lord.'"

This verse is another clear example showing that the Jews and Christians had the Word of God in their possession prior to the writing of the Qur'an. Since Jews and Christians are commanded by Surah 5:68 to observe the precepts contained in their Scripture, it would have been impossible for them to know the commandments they must obey if their Book had perished. Or if the

Bible had been previously corrupted, they would have gone astray if they obeyed it.

There is no indication in the Qur'an whatsoever that the Holy Scriptures the Jews and Christians had in their possession were anything other than the original Holy Books God had revealed to them.

Surah 5:68, which we just mentioned, is another clear example that Islam, as recorded in the Qur'an, did not and should not abrogate the Christian faith that preceded it. On the contrary, the Qur'an commands all Jewish and Christian believers to follow their Holy Scriptures.

Because the Qur'an testifies that the Holy Scripture of the Jews and Christians is the Word of God, the Muslim should submit to the authority of the Qur'an on this point. The Muslim should look no further. If the words of Muslim teachers or even Traditions (Hadith)[1] contradict what the Qur'an states, the true Muslim should follow the Qur'an because the Qur'an is much higher in authority according to Islamic law and beliefs.

Early Muslim Scholars Uphold Bible Integrity

Al-Ghazzali (AD 1058–1111), is considered one of the greatest Muslim theologians in the history of Islam. In his writings he never challenged the Bible's integrity. He even wrote treatises on the Trinity in which he quoted many passages from the Bible, without questioning the trustworthiness of the text.[2]

Al-Tabari, one of the earliest authoritative commentators on the Qur'an, comments on Surah 5:68. He noted that Ibn Abbas, one of Muhammad's companions, said that some Jews wanted to know if Muhammad believed the Torah. And so they asked Muhammad,

"Oh Muhammad, do you not claim that you walk in the steps of Abraham's Community and religion, and do you not believe in The Torah which we have and confess that it is God's truth?"

The messenger [Muhammad] said, "Of course I do but you have read into the Scripture things that are not there and you have rejected God's Covenant with you. You have concealed what you had been commanded to make known to the people. Therefore, I disown your innovations."

They replied, "We abide by what is in our hands [The Torah]; we follow the truth and the guidance and we do not believe in you nor do we follow you."[3]

Here we see that Muhammad admits that the Torah is God's truth, but accuses the Jews of concealing its teaching.

Many Traditions (Ahadith) record that when Muhammad was asked to judge on some disputes, he asked for the Torah to be read aloud to him. These Traditions are further evidence that Muhammad considered the Torah to be holy and uncorrupted.

For example, I read in the most acknowledged biography on Muhammad's life, by Ibn Hisham, a story about a man and a woman who were caught in adultery. In that story, the people asked Muhammad to be the judge. Muhammad asked a rabbi to read the passage about adultery.

As the rabbi read from the Torah, Abdullah B. Salam struck the rabbi's hand saying, "This, oh prophet of God, is the verse of stoning which he refuses to read to you." Muhammad then said, "Woe to you Jews! What has induced you to abandon the judgment of God which you hold in your hands?"[4]

THE IMPORTANCE OF READING THE GOSPEL

My dear Muslim reader, to enjoy a right and complete relationship with God, you must read the Gospel (the New Testament). It will increase your understanding of Jesus Christ (Al-Masih, Isa). It will also help you to understand the salvation God wants you to experience through faith in Him.

The Qur'an mentions the glad news of Jesus in Surah 3:45 "Behold! The angel said: 'O Mary! Allah giveth thee Glad Tidings of a Word from him: His name will be Christ Jesus . . ."

2

WAS THE BIBLE ALTERED, AS SOME MUSLIMS CLAIM?

My dear Muslim reader, it is only fair that you examine the evidence with objectivity. Any accusation that the Bible was altered raises serious questions, which demand answers from those people who have made this claim. When could this alleged alteration of the Holy Scriptures have occurred?

A. Before Muhammad's time?
   All the verses pointed out in the previous chapter clearly demonstrate that Muhammad did not believe the Bible to be corrupt in his time.
B. After the death of Muhammad?
   It is not possible for the Bible to have been altered after the death of Muhammad because by AD 600 Christianity had spread as far as Asia, Africa, and Europe.

COMPARISONS OF BIBLE
TRANSLATIONS REVEAL TEXTUAL ACCURACY

Those who had embraced Christianity in Asia, Africa, and Europe had no common language. The Bible was circulating in many different languages around the world. This would make any attempt to falsify the Holy Scriptures impossible, and comparisons of these Bible translations in the various languages reveal complete accuracy of the Bible text.

An Impossible Conspiracy

It is not rational to suppose that Christians and Jews throughout the world could meet and agree on the alterations of their Holy Scripture. History shows that Jews and Christians have had major doctrinal differences between them, and they have been in disagreement regarding many religious issues. (See Surah 2:113.)

We also read in many verses in the Qur'an that Christians were divided into sects. So if the Scriptures had been changed to alter doctrine, at least one of the many sects that existed within Judaism or Christianity at that time would have protested. Yet there is no historical mention of any such accusation or dissension.

By the time Muhammad lived, Christianity had spread throughout the world. Therefore, it would have been impossible for anyone or any group to collect all the Holy Books, manuscripts, and writings containing scriptural references from all the churches, synagogues, schools, libraries, and homes to make the changes. Then the replacements would have had to be returned without detection. How could everyone who had a Bible be convinced to exchange it for a corrupted version, and yet leave no evidence of such a monumental feat?

More Evidence for Textual Purity of the Bible

Many sincere Christian scholars during the time of Muhammad, such as the Abyssinians who loved Muslims and befriended them, would have exposed any attempted changes in the Scriptures.

Surah 5:82 describes these Christians. It reads: "Strongest among men in enmity to the believers wilt thou find the Jews and pagans; and nearest among them in love to the believers wilt thou find those who say: 'We are Christians' because amongst these are men devoted to learning and men who have renounced the world, and they are not arrogant."

Note that this verse describes these Christians as "devoted to learning." Since these dedicated Christians knew very well the revelations given to them from God, they would have discovered any attempted tampering. The verse also describes these Christians: "They have renounced the world, and they are not arrogant," which means these Christians were living a godly life. Therefore, they would not have committed such a terrible sin of changing or corrupting their Holy Scriptures.

Lack of Evidence for Textual Corruption

Surah 5:66, which states, "There is from among them a party on the right course," shows that there were a significant number of Jews and Christians who did not compromise, but were faithful and stood fast by the Law and the Gospel. Such a steadfast group would have exposed any attempt to corrupt their Holy Scriptures.

In addition, from Muhammad's time forward, many Jews and Christians in lands conquered by the Muslim army embraced Islam. Since Muslims revered the Holy Books of the Jews and the Christians, the Jews and Christians who became Muslims would have retained their reverence for their original Scriptures as well.

Yet no texts have been discovered that differ from today's Bible.

If the Jews and Christians had collaborated to corrupt the Bible, surely some of these Muslim converts would have been able to produce unaltered copies of the Holy Books. In fact, hundreds of manuscripts exist today from the fourth and fifth centuries (Islam started in the sixth century). These manuscripts agree with today's translations of the Scripture (Injeel). Any variances are minor and do not affect any essential doctrine. So the New Testament of Muhammad's day is the same as the New Testament today. This is a well-established fact that is widely agreed upon.

Challenging the Basis for the Accusations

These circumstances render it impossible for Jews and Christians to have come together after the death of Muhammad to alter their Holy Scriptures. Those Muslims who claim that today's Bible is altered or corrupt need to answer the following questions:

- When and where did this corruption take place?
- Who were the perpetrators?
- How did they reach a consensus?
- If there were an original Bible different from the one that exists today, where is it so that we can make a comparison? What specific textual changes were made to the original manuscripts?
- What evidence proves any alterations of doctrines?

ACCORDING TO GOD, THE BIBLE CANNOT CHANGE

The Word of God is unchangeable as God originally presented it in the Holy Scriptures of the Jews and the Christians. The Qur'an itself asserts repeatedly that no one can alter the

Word of God. Surah 6:34 states, "There is none that can alter the Words (and Decrees) of Allah." Surah 10:64 states, "No change can there be in the Words of Allah." Both Surah 6:115 and Surah 18:27 state, "None can change His Words."

In addition, the Bible emphasizes that the Word of God does not change. In the Old Testament, Isaiah 40:8 reads, "The grass withers and the flowers fall, but the word of our God endures forever."

Jesus said, "Heaven and earth will pass away, but my words will never pass away" (Matthew 24:35).

Therefore, whoever claims that the Bible is corrupted or changed calls God a liar and actually accuses God of being unable to protect and preserve His Word.

When any of my Muslim acquaintances or friends tell me, "The Bible is corrupted," I reply, "God forbid," or in Arabic, "Astaghfar Allah."

The Earliest Revelation Is the Foundation

We know counterfeit currency can be made after the authorized one is first given. What is the standard that we use to examine currency to see if it is authentic or counterfeit? Do we use the original authorized currency or a recent one? Obviously the same principle applies when we ask if a book is God's Word or not. Of course the standard should be the earlier holy books not the most recent book.

Therefore, it is not possible, as some Muslims claim, that God first sent the Torah, the Zabor (Psalms), and the Injeel (the Gospel), and then allowed them to be corrupted.

Even the Qur'an indicates harmony with this principle. For in Surah 10:94 a command is given to Muhammad and all Muslims to treat the Bible as the primary source of enlightenment.

The verse reads, "If thou wert in doubt as to what We have revealed unto thee then ask those who have been reading the Book from before thee."

HOW COULD IT POSSIBLY BENEFIT THE JEWS OR THE CHRISTIANS TO CORRUPT HOLY SCRIPTURES?

What purpose or benefit would it have been to the Christians and the Jews to corrupt their own Holy Scriptures? Why then would they continue to believe their Scripture? If they had done this, how could they bring themselves to pass it on to their children? Such an allegation is irrational.

Some Muslims claim the Bible may have contained prophecies related to Muhammad and that they were deleted. Where is the evidence? If such prophecies were originally found in the Bible, Christians and Jews would have acknowledged Muhammad. They would have followed him and benefited by sharing in the spoils given to Muslims at the conquests of Persia, Syria, Palestine, Egypt, and many other lands.

In the Torah, God warned the Jews, "Do not add to what I command you and do not subtract from it, but keep the commands of the LORD your God that I give you" (Deuteronomy 4:2). (See also Deuteronomy 12:32.) If such prophecies about Muhammad did exist, why would Jews and Christians bring upon themselves and their beloved children sufferings here on earth and forever by eliminating those prophecies? In fact, the temptation would be greater to try to find prophecies of Muhammad rather than to eliminate any. For example, by becoming Muslims they could have avoided a disadvantaged status as a minority at the time when Muhammad died and Islam was spreading rapidly through conquest.

Also, when you read the Bible, you will find many statements and paragraphs that show the bad actions and sins of many Jewish religious leaders and people.

It does not make any sense that Jews corrupted the Bible without deleting all the negative words that still exist all over the Bible against them.

3

THE GOSPEL IS
GOD'S GLAD NEWS

While I was talking with one of my dear Muslim friends, he told me the Qur'an mentions only one Gospel, but the Bible has four Gospels. I answered, "The word *gospel* refers to the glad news of God's love toward everyone, which came to us through Jesus Christ. Gospel means 'good news.' It is interesting to read in the Qur'an, "Behold!" The angels said: "Oh Mary! Allah giveth thee glad tidings of a Word from Him: his name will be Christ Jesus" (Surah 3:45).

The glad news provided in the Gospel for the human race was written by clear revelation from God. It shows us how we can be saved from hell and enjoy eternal life with God.

THE LIVING REVELATION OF GOD

We know from reading the Bible that Jesus Christ, a living person, is the perfect revelation of God to the human race. We read in the Gospel that "Jesus went throughout Galilee . . . proclaiming the good news [gospel] of the kingdom, and healing every disease and sickness among the people" (Matthew 4:23). Thereafter, Jesus commanded His disciples to proclaim the gospel (the good news which He revealed to them) to all the people of the world. (See Acts 1:8 and Matthew 28:18–20.)

The Gospel tells us that the Messiah, the Savior who was foretold by the prophets, has come. (See John 1:45.)

Divine Inspiration Comes from the Holy Spirit

There is only one Gospel and only one Messiah, Jesus. God inspired Jesus' apostles through the guidance of the Holy Spirit to tell us about the person, life, and teachings of Jesus. The Bible states: "All Scripture is God-breathed and is useful for teaching, rebuking, correcting and training in righteousness, so that the servant of God may be thoroughly equipped for every good work" (2 Timothy 3:16–17). This verse means God "breathed" His words and thoughts through His selected messengers. God is the ultimate Author of the message and doctrines of the Gospel.

We read in the Bible, "Knowing this first, that no prophecy of Scripture is of any private interpretation, for prophecy never came by the will of man, but holy men of God spoke as they were moved by the Holy Spirit" (2 Peter 1:20–21 NKJV). It is clear that the Holy Spirit moved men to write each word as revealed by God.

More than two thousand times in the Old Testament alone, there are clauses such as, "God spoke to Moses" and "God said, 'The Word of the Lord came unto Jonah,'" and many more.

Four Presentations of the One Gospel of God

If we had only one account of the life of Jesus, many people would be suspicious and wonder if the one account were true. God gave us four accounts written by four separate and distinct individuals. Matthew and John were eyewitnesses and two of

Jesus' twelve disciples. Luke, a historian (Luke 1:1–4), received his information from eyewitnesses (Luke 1:2). Mark spent extensive time with Peter, one of Jesus' closest friends who witnessed all the major events in His life.

Four followers of Christ, Matthew, Mark, Luke, and John, wrote testimonies of Jesus' life and recorded His teachings. None of their writings contradict. All their writings proclaim the glad news of God's love shown through Jesus. Each writer simply tells the story in a different way.

Jesus assured the Gospel writers that the Holy Spirit would guide each one's writings and remind them of what He had spoken. "The Helper, the Holy Spirit, whom the Father will send in My name, He will teach you all things, and bring to your remembrance all things that I said to you" (John 14:26 NKJV).

My dear reader, when you study the Gospel as recorded by John, you are studying the glad news of the kingdom of God as taught by Jesus. John, who was inspired by the Holy Spirit and a close companion of Jesus, could easily keep notes of His teachings.

John was an eyewitness to the death, resurrection, and ascension of Jesus, as were Matthew and nine other disciples.

The apostle John assures us that the disciples actually walked and talked with Jesus:

> That which was from the beginning [Jesus], which we have heard, which we have seen with our eyes, which we have looked at and our hands have touched—this we proclaim concerning the Word of life. The life appeared; we have seen it and testify to it. (1 John 1:1–3)

God guided His writers to accurately record what happened (Luke 1:1–4). Their writings precisely connect with actual historical events.

All of the disciples wrote one message, which is the gospel of Jesus Christ. Jesus even prophesied seventeen times about the spreading of the gospel (e.g., Matthew 24:14).

Other New Testament Writings

In addition to the four presentations of the Gospel, the New Testament also contains inspired teachings and letters written by apostles and disciples of Jesus to different groups of Christians and ultimately to all believers. The apostle Paul said, "For I received from the Lord what I also passed on to you" (1 Corinthians 11:23). (See also 1 Thessalonians 2:13.)

Some of my Muslim friends ask me, "Did you know that the apostle Paul created the teaching that Jesus is God?" I usually ask them, "Why would he do that? What did he have to profit?" It is recorded in history and in the New Testament that Paul used to persecute Christians (Acts 9); he was an educated, powerful Jewish leader with tremendous authority to arrest, persecute, and even kill Christians. He lost all his authority and prestige for Jesus' sake. Paul became poor and suffered greatly, even risking his life many times to help people know Jesus (2 Corinthians 11:23–27).

All the words written in the New Testament are significant echoes of Jesus' teachings. They help us to grow morally and spiritually.

Peter makes known to us that the apostles were actual eyewitnesses to the life of Jesus. Peter declared, "For we did not follow cleverly devised stories when we told you about the coming of our Lord Jesus Christ in power, but we were eyewitnesses of his majesty" (2 Peter 1:16).

The whole New Testament was written soon after Jesus' death (AD 40–96). In about AD 42, Jesus' disciples were called Christians (Acts 11:26). Some Muslims wonder where the name "Christian" came from. The letters "ian" in those days meant "belonging to."

So the followers of Jesus were called Christians because every-body knew that they belonged to Christ.

Different Translations of the Bible

A notable fact is that Muslim scholars consider only the Arabic Qur'an to be the actual Word of God. Any translation of the Arabic Qur'an to a different language is not considered to be the actual Word of God.

Muslim teachers insist that believers must learn Arabic and pray in Arabic because it is the language of God. However, all Christian scholars agree that praying in Arabic is not necessary because God understands all languages.

Some Muslim scholars point to the different translations of the Bible to prove that it could not be the Word of God.

We disagree with them because we know that the most divine thing in the Bible is not certain words or expressions, but actually the meaning of these words. The divine inspiration is in the meaning, not in specific language. God does not require all people to study and excel in one language in order to understand His Word.

God does not desire us to be slaves to the letter but to under-stand and live His will.

Biblical scholar David W. Shenk explains *divine inspiration*. He wrote:

Divine inspiration does not mean Divine dictation. Christians do not believe that the prophets who spoke or wrote the Word of God were [mindless] tubes through which God's words flowed. In all of the biblical scriptures, the personality of the different writers is evident. . . . God's inspiring activity does not cancel human involvement in the process. The imprint of human personality is part of the content of biblical revelation.

... The Bible is the marvelous drama of God revealing Himself to persons, and the inspired prophets of God expressing that revelation in human language and thought forms.[1]

The Old Testament was written in Hebrew with a few chapters in Aramaic. And the New Testament was written in Greek. Converting those languages into English or any other language is referred to as a translation. Followers of Christ recognize the credibility of a translation of the Bible as long as it retains the teaching and the meaning found in the original language.

With the passage of time, words change in meaning. Words continue to slowly fall in and out of use. New translations of the Bible have helped a variety of people to understand more clearly the Word of God in their contemporary languages.

None of these new translations conflict with any doctrinal teaching. The differences between these translations are relatively insignificant.

A typo in a copy of the Bible or an inaccurate translation of a word or a passage cannot be used as proof that the Bible is corrupted. In the same way a scratch in a Mercedes car does not mean the car is no longer a genuine Mercedes.

There are several different English translations of the Arabic Qur'an. For example, Surah 19:88, as translated by Yusuf Ali, says:

"They say: (Allah) Most Gracious has begotten a son!"

But Pickthal and Daryebadi in their translations use the word "taken" instead of begotten.

My Muslim friend, the most important proof that the Gospel is the divine Word of God comes when it is prayerfully read. God's Word will enlighten your mind and God will knock softly on the door of your heart. He will truly speak to you and change your life!

The words of Jesus and His disciples in the New Testament contain the highest moral standards ever said and written, which is strong evidence that the words came from God. The Bible is not a Christian or Jewish book. It is God's Word sent from God through His prophets to all people.

THE CERTAINTY OF THE BIBLE

The word "Bible" is taken from the Greek word *biblia*, which means "book." The Bible is divided into two parts: the Old Testament books and the New Testament books. The word "testament" means "covenant," which refers to the relationship between God and His people. The Old Testament contains the Torah, the Psalms, and the books of the Prophets.

Hundreds of books present conclusive evidence that demonstrate the authenticity and reliability of the Bible. One popular book is *The New Evidence That Demands a Verdict*, by Josh McDowell.[2]

You may be asking, "How do I know with *certainty* that any writing is from God?" Test it. The Bible warns its readers to "test everything that is said. Hold on to what is good" (1 Thessalonians 5:21 NLT).

Regardless of the opinions of friends or family, our own individual destiny lies in the balance. Our choice of a holy book should be carefully and prayerfully considered. God has given us minds to test such things. To refuse to use our God-given minds because of pressures from others would be fearing created beings more than the *Creator*! So what kind of test is there to see if something is supernaturally inspired by God? There are two key tests:

1. Is It *Prophetic* with Accuracy?

This question is the most important test. In the Bible, God revealed that the test for true prophecy is that it must be fulfilled with 100 percent accuracy. Prophets who were not 100 percent accurate were deemed false and were to be stoned to death (Deuteronomy 18:20).

2. Is It *Reliable*?

The evidence for reliability of the biblical manuscripts far exceeds the evidence for all other ancient writings. Researchers Geisler and Nix conclude, "In contrast to the total number of over 5,000 New Testament manuscripts known today, other religious and historical books of the ancient world pale in significance."[3] Two classic books: *From God to Us: How We Got Our Bible*, by Norman Geisler and William Nix, and *The New Testament Documents: Are They Reliable?* by F. F. Bruce,[4] provide evidence for the trustworthiness of the Bible.

PROPHETIC PROOF

In the Bible, God declares that He is outside of time. "I am God, and there is no other; I am God, and there is none like me. I make known the end from the beginning, from ancient times, what is still to come" (Isaiah 46:9–10).

To test any supposed holy work, the first consideration should be to find proof. Are words proofs? Of course not, for any word can be alleged to be true. Is belief proof? No, because people can be taught from childhood to believe in wrong teachings.

However, if someone could always foretell the future with total accuracy, that is, the specific predictions are always fulfilled and historically verifiable, it would establish that the information came from God. Only *God* possesses the ability to know fully what is to come.

Throughout this book, you will discover some of the many amazing, specific prophecies in the Holy Scriptures of the Jews concerning Jesus' birth, life, ministry, crucifixion, death, and resurrection. These prophecies were written hundreds of years before Jesus' birth. Each one of them was fulfilled in the life of Christ.

Archeology

Archeology affirms the accuracy of the Bible. In 1974, *Time* magazine published an article that stated, "After more than two centuries of facing the heaviest scientific guns that could be brought to bear, the Bible has survived, and is perhaps better for the siege. Even on the critic's own terms, historical fact, the scriptures seem more acceptable now than when the rationalists began the attack."

Archeological findings by both Christians and non-Christians have confirmed the reliability and the accuracy of the biblical writers regarding numerous customs, names, places, and events. (See *Halley's Bible Handbook* for artifacts.[5])

Only the Bible amazingly predicts precise historical events centuries in advance of their fulfillment. These prophecies are supported by archaeological evidence.

In about AD 32, Jesus predicted the destruction of the city of Jerusalem. (See Luke 19:43–44.) Just as Jesus had predicted, in AD 70 the Roman general Titus destroyed Jerusalem.

Scientific Prophecies

Another form of prophecy is the scientific information found in the Bible. These facts was given to biblical authors two thousand years or more before modern science discovered them. For example, the Bible records that the earth is round (Isaiah 40:22). And God "hangs the earth on nothing" (Job 26:7 NKJV). Today, we know these are facts.

In his book *Science and the Bible*, Dr. Henry Morris identifies many of the scientific prophecies found in the Bible.[6]

Regarding biology, hydrology, geology, etc., and how they correlate with scientific facts known today, this fascinating book gives detailed information on these prophesied scientific facts.

Many religious leaders have claimed that their words were from God, but *none* have stood the test of complete and accurate prophecy. Only the Bible passes this test. Its detailed, fulfilled, historical prophecies provide evidence for its authenticity without a doubt. You will read throughout this book more about fulfilled prophecies. Another excellent reference is *Every Prophecy of the Bible,* by John F. Walvoord.[7]

THE TESTIMONY OF THE ANCIENT MANUSCRIPTS

Today Christians have in their possession many ancient manuscripts of the Bible that date back many generations before Muhammad started the Islamic religion and before the Qur'an was written. Today's modern Bible does not differ from these ancient biblical manuscripts.

Codex Vaticanus (dated AD 325–350)

The Codex Vaticanus manuscript includes all of the books of the Bible up to the New Testament book of Hebrews (9:14).[8] The remaining portion of the New Testament is included by a later writer.[9] Codex Vaticanus is currently located in the Vatican library.

Codex Alexandrinus (dated AD 400)

The Codex Alexandrinus manuscript contains almost the entire Bible. This preserved manuscript is kept in the British Museum.[10]

Codex Sinaiticus (dated AD 350)

The Codex Sinaiticus manuscript contains the entire New Testament and a portion of the Old Testament. It is also found in the British Museum.[11]

The fact that these manuscripts existed at least two hundred years before Muhammad founded Islam means that the only Holy Book in the hands of the Christians at Muhammad's time consisted of the same Old and New Testaments we have today.

The Septuagint

The Septuagint is the Greek translation of the Hebrew Holy Scriptures, the Old Testament.[12] It was completed almost three hundred years before Christ was born. This translation contains all the prophecies of the coming Messiah that Jesus fulfilled when He came. The Septuagint, which is well documented in Jewish and secular history, shows consistent accuracy with today's Old Testament.

4

DID MUHAMMAD COME TO ESTABLISH A NEW RELIGION?

Many Muslim teachers claim that Muhammad's mission was to establish a new religion. However, according to the Qur'an itself, Muhammad's mission was not to establish a new religion but to preserve the religion of Abraham in the Torah (Old Testament). Some such Qur'anic passages are:

"Say: 'Allah speaketh the Truth: follow the religion of Abraham...'" (Surah 3:95)

"Who can be better in religion than one who submits his whole self to Allah, does good, and follows the way of Abraham the true in faith? For Allah did take Abraham for a friend." (Surah 4:125)

"So we have taught thee [Muhammad] the inspired (message), 'Follow the ways of Abraham the True in Faith.'" (Surah 16:123; see Surah 6:161)

As proved earlier, the Qur'an never states that its words replaced the words of the previous Holy Scriptures of the Jews and Christians. The Qur'an does state that some of its verses abrogate other verses in the Qur'an. (See Surah 2:106 and 16:101.)

THE QUR'AN ITSELF SAYS MUHAMMAD DID NOT COME TO TEACH NEW DOCTRINES

As I showed you in chapter one, the Qur'an frequently affirms that Muhammad was given revelations to confirm what was already revealed in the Holy Books of the Jews and Christians. It does not claim to correct, replace, add to, or annul the Bible. Let me mention some Qur'anic passages as a confirmation:

"Nothing is said to thee [Muhammad] that was not said to the Messengers before thee." (Surah 41:43)

"The same religion has He [God] established for you as that which He enjoined on Noah . . . and that which we enjoined on Abraham, Moses, and Jesus: namely, that ye should remain steadfast in Religion, and make no divisions therein." (Surah 42:13)

"Say [Muhammad]: 'I am no bringer of new-fangled doctrine among the messengers, nor do I know what will be done with me or with you.'" (Surah 46:9)

"Muhammad is no more than a Messenger: many were the Messengers that passed away before him." (Surah 3:144)

"Say [Muhammad]: 'It is not in my power to cause you harm, or to bring you to right conduct..'" (Surah 72:21)

"Say: 'I am but a man like yourselves . . .'" (Surah 18:110)

WHO WAS THE QUR'AN INTENDED FOR?

Some verses in the Qur'an indicate that the Qur'an was given for the people of Mecca. For example, "Thus have We sent by inspiration to thee an Arabic Qur'an: That thou mayest warn the Mother of Cities and all around her." (Surah 42:7).

We read in the Qur'an that it is for Arabic speaking people. For example:

"We have sent it down as an Arabic Qur'an, in order that ye may learn wisdom." (Surah 12:2)

"A Book, whereof the verses are explained in detail—A Qur'an in Arabic, for people who understand." (Surah 41:3)

"We have made it a Qur'an in Arabic, that ye may be able to understand." (Surah 43:3)

"Verily, We have made This [Qur'an] easy, in thy tongue, in order that they may give heed." (Surah 44:58)

"And before this, was the Book of Moses as a guide and a mercy: And this Book confirms (it) in the Arabic tongue . . ." (Surah 46:12)

SUBMISSION TO GOD
WITHOUT FOLLOWING MUHAMMAD

It is significant that even, according to the Qur'an, believers in God submitted their lives to Him without following Muhammad or the teachings of the Qur'an.

According to the Qur'an, the followers of Jesus are superior and people should follow Jesus until the last day. The Qur'an states: "Behold! Allah said: O Jesus! . . . I will make those who follow thee superior to those who reject faith, to the Day of Resurrection" (Surah 3:55).

The Qur'an states that Abraham and Jacob submitted their lives to God (Surah 2:131–133). It is well known that the Qur'an classified Jesus (Isa) and all the prophets as ones who submit their lives to God (Surah 2:136). The Qur'an also describes the followers of Jesus as ones who submit their lives to God (Surah 3:52). (See also Surah 5:111.)

According to the Qur'an, a Muslim is one who submits his whole self to God and is a doer of good. It is significant that a person can submit his life to God without following Muhammad or the Qur'an.

My dear Muslim reader, when you read the Bible, you will discover that the true believers in God and followers of Jesus Christ are called to surrender their lives completely and submit their whole being to the One and only living God, the Creator of heaven and earth. This is the clear teaching of Jesus and His disciples. The Bible urges believers to submit themselves to God (James 4:7).

My precious reader, you can submit your life to God through believing in Jesus and following His teaching.

The believers who truly submit their lives to God are brave enough to live by what God has revealed in the Holy Scriptures. They do not follow the opinions of men or tradition (Hadith) that contradict the clear revelation of God.

Also, genuine believers do not follow their own preference or their own interpretation. They keep all the words of God in their hearts and minds and ask God continually to guide them. They establish their beliefs based on balanced assimilation of the Word of God.

AN INVITATION

My dear reader, are you burdened, worried, or lonely? Do you feel spiritually or emotionally thirsty? The God of the Bible does not desire for you to live life this way. Jesus offers a comforting invitation: "Let anyone who is thirsty, come to me and drink" (John 7:37).

As physical water satisfies your body, Jesus promised that He will satisfy your heart.

ADAM IN THE QUR'AN AND IN THE BIBLE

5

ADAM IN ISLAM

My dear reader, this section is exciting because it reveals the desire of God's heart, which is to fellowship with people and to relate to us personally!

ADAM CREATED PERFECT BY GOD

The Qur'an states that God created Adam in a perfect condition. We read in Surah 95:4, "We have indeed created man in the best of moulds." Surah 2:30 states that Adam was God's representative ("Khalifah").[1] In addition, we read in Surah 15:29, "When I have fashioned him [Adam] and breathed into him of My Spirit . . ."

ADAM AND EVE PLACED IN PERFECT CIRCUMSTANCES

According to the Qur'an, God gave Adam and Eve perfect circumstances. He created them in the heavenly garden. God gave them everything they needed to enjoy and live a righteous life. Surah 2:35 states: "We said: 'O Adam! Dwell thou and thy wife in the Garden [Jannatu], and eat of the bountiful things therein as (where and when) ye will . . .'"

GOD'S DESIRE TO COMMUNICATE PERSONALLY WITH US

We read in Surah 2:31: "And He [God] taught Adam the names of all things." This verse indicates that God spoke in human voice and talked to Adam many times and Adam had a personal, direct, and wonderful relationship with God. According to the Qur'an, Adam and Eve were able to enjoy perfect fellowship with God. As you will clearly see, it was the original intention of the almighty, transcendent God to personally connect with the people He created because He is gracious and humble.

SATAN TEMPTED ADAM AND EVE, AND THEY FELL

God placed a certain tree in the middle of the garden and gave Adam and Eve the freedom to eat from any tree in the garden except this one tree.

We read in the Qur'an a clear warning to Adam: "We said: 'O Adam! Dwell thou and thy wife in the Garden; and eat of the bountiful things therein . . . but approach not this tree, or ye run into harm and transgression'" (Surah 2:35).

Adam and Eve chose to disobey God and ate fruit from the forbidden tree. As soon as they disobeyed God, they were cast out of the garden.

The Qur'an states that Satan tempted and deceived Adam and Eve and that they failed to represent God. They disobeyed God and sinned. "They both ate of the tree, Thus did Adam disobey his Lord, and allowed himself to be seduced" (Surah 20:121).

The Qur'an described what happened in Surah 2:36: "Then did Satan make them slip from the (Garden) and get them out of the state (of felicity) in which they had been. We said: 'Get ye down, all (ye people), with enmity between yourselves. On earth will be your dwelling place.'"

The Arabic Qur'an named the place where Adam and Eve lived before they disobeyed God as "Jannatu" (the English translation is "garden"), which is the same name that the Qur'an gives to heaven. (See Surah 9:72.)

There is a strong indication in the Qur'an that Adam and Eve were created in heaven itself and enjoyed peace and felicity until they disobeyed God and were cast out of heaven.

GOD'S PENALTY EXTENDED TO ALL MANKIND

Note that in Surah 2:36, the form used in Arabic is the imperative *ahbituu*, "get ye down," which means "get down, descend, crash down."[2] The widely acclaimed Muslim scholar and commentator of the Qur'an, Pickthall, says, "Here the command is in the plural, as addressed to Adam's race."[3]

Abdullah Yusuf Ali explained the phrase "Get ye down, all (ye people)" (Surah 2:36), in his popular translation and commentary of the Qur'an: "Allah's decree is the result of man's action. Note the transition in Arabic from the singular number in Surah 2:33 to the dual in Surah 2:35 and the plural here, which I have indicated in English by 'All ye people.' Evidently Adam is the type of all mankind."[4]

The Qur'an teaches the fall of Adam and implicates the whole human race in this fall. In Surah 2:38, we read that the same command given to Adam and Eve was given to their offspring: "Get ye down all [jamean] from here."

Note the Arabic word *jamean* is taken to mean a "host, congregation, all, together, altogether."[5] Therefore, God's command to depart from the garden was intended not only for Adam and

Eve, but also for all their descendants. This verse points to the fact that mankind as a whole was affected by the disobedience of Adam and Eve. The Hadith confirms this truth.[6]

Adam was the first human created. He is the father of all humankind. We all originate from him. His disobedience affected all the members of his family. It is from this point of origin that mankind has had to face its ultimate problem—the result of Adam's fall into sin.

6

THE RESULTS OF THE FALL

According to the Gospel, when God created man, His purpose was that man might enjoy constant and beautiful fellowship with Him.

ADAM'S SIN SEPARATED HIM FROM GOD

God's intention for man was being fulfilled while Adam walked in fellowship with Him. But Adam disobeyed God. Adam's relationship with God was broken as a result of sin.[1] The prophet Isaiah declared, "Surely the arm of the LORD is not too short to save, nor his ear too dull to hear. But your iniquities have separated you from your God" (59:1–2). Adam's sin and our sin caused the separation between mankind and the holy God.

Adam was created morally pure. When he disobeyed God he lost the ability to be completely moral, which is known as the Fall.

ADAM CHOSE TO REBEL

God placed a certain tree in the middle of the garden as a symbol of His authority over man. Adam was granted the freedom to choose. The moment Adam and Eve chose to eat the fruit from the forbidden tree, they intentionally challenged and violated the authority of God. Their sin was an act of defiance against the authority of Almighty God. Because Adam and Eve ate of the forbidden fruit, God expelled them from the garden.

No one can make light of Adam's sin by saying he just forgot God's command. Adam could not have possibly forgotten the only command God gave him, especially since Satan had just reminded him of God's prohibition (Surah 7:20).

SIN INFECTED ALL HUMANITY

The original sin of Adam and Eve had a devastating effect on the whole human race. Sin entered the human nature. The effect of their sin became universal and all humanity now plunges into a world where sin and death reign. My dear friend, sin became an integral part of human nature.

God created man in His own image and gave him the freedom of choice. Man chose to rebel against God. Consequently, Adam's sin distorted God's image in mankind. The human nature fell captive to the power of sin and became intrinsically corrupt. Man cannot purify his soul to the state it was in before the fall. Even Muhammad said, "Satan runs in the body of Adam's son [i.e., man] as his blood circulates in it."[2]

I was discussing the topic of Adam with a Muslim acquaintance and he responded, "This is not fair and does not make any sense that we suffer because of Adam and Eve's wrong choice and their disobedience to God." I explained to him that this principle

THE RESULTS OF THE FALL

is logical and observable even today. For example, when a leader wages war, people are killed; a whole country can suffer from its leader's wrong decision. Another example is when parents live an immoral lifestyle and their children suffer because of their parents' wrong choices.

These types of instances have been repeated among mankind since the beginning.

ADAM'S SIN TAINTED HUMAN NATURE

Sin permanently tainted human nature. Fallen humanity experiences sin's effect daily through self-centeredness, jealousy, envy, hate, etc.

According to the following verses in the Qur'an, all humans are captive to the power of sin:

Surah 12:53, "The (human) soul is certainly prone to evil."

Surah 16:61, "If Allah were to punish men for their wrongdoing, He would not leave, on the (earth), a single living creature."

Muhammad said: "Every son of Adam is a sinner."[3] Surely all of us can testify that we are prone to indulge ourselves. At times we violate our conscience and yield to our selfish nature, which is sin. Even within the best of all human hearts remains an evil nature.

THE DEVASTATING CONSEQUENCES OF SIN

God created Adam as a perfect human being who would live forever. Man was not originally created to die. He was not originally programmed for death. God warned Adam of the devastating consequences of sin, "For when you eat from it you will certainly die" (Genesis 2:17).

Sin sentenced us to a slow death. We were like flowers planted in God's garden. Sin cut us off from God's presence like a flower plucked from its source of life. It is just a matter of time before that flower dies completely.

We need a miracle. And the practice of religious duties and rituals cannot bring us life. We need Someone who can give us life.

Sin prevents a person from enjoying God's presence and from having a personal relationship with God. Because of our sinful condition and the sins we commit, all of our being—our body, spirit, and soul—is separated from God now and forever. And no amount of works or efforts sinners can do will reverse the effects and consequences of their sin, and they cannot bridge the distance between them and God.

The Bible states, "Sin entered the world through one man, and death through sin, and in this way death came to all people, because all sinned" (Romans 5:12). All men continue to sin because sin is now an integral part of human nature.

It is apparent that the circumstances of life did not bring sin to man, but rather it is man who brought sin to the world. It is clear that the descendants of Adam inherited all the characteristics of his fallen nature. As a consequence, we all became subject to the condemnation of God because of the sins we committed against Him. He is holy and righteous and cannot tolerate sin. God's law and justice are stated in the Bible: "The wages of sin is death" (Romans 6:23).

7

RECONCILIATION IS POSSIBLE

God's eternal love for mankind did not change because of man's disobedience. God planned a way to save mankind, to restore our relationship with Him. God's holiness demanded justice and punishment toward sinners, while His immeasurable love pleaded for mercy and forgiveness for them. The God of the Bible has not stood still. He came to us in the person of Jesus Christ! Therefore, Jesus Christ (the Living Word of God) became flesh and, on the cross, suffered the consequences of our sin. God's total judgment against sin fell upon Jesus.

In Jesus, we see an accurate picture of the balance between God's righteous anger and God's love.

On our behalf, Christ voluntarily paid the price we should have paid for all the sins we have committed, and ever will commit, against God. Christ loves each one of us. The apostle Paul said Jesus "loved me and gave himself for me" (Galatians 2:20).

The moment you believe that Jesus paid the penalty for everything wrong you did and repent of your sins by telling

God that you do want to obey Him, you will be reconciled with God.

JESUS, THE ONLY SINLESS, PERFECT MAN

The Gospel, in Luke 4, teaches that Satan tempted Jesus to act independently from God's will and offered to give Him the kingdoms of the world if He worshiped him. Unlike Adam and Eve, who broke their relationship with God through their disobedience, Jesus had complete victory over Satan's temptations to sin. In the Gospel, Jesus is recognized as the perfect man who submitted every moment of His life to the will of God.

All other people throughout human history have yielded to Satan's temptations and have sinned regularly. Jesus was the only exception. According to the teaching of both the Qur'an and the Gospel, Jesus was the only man to live a life without committing one single sin.

Because Jesus alone lived His life in perfect obedience to God, He is the only One able to restore us to a right relationship with God.

YOU NEED TO BECOME SPIRITUALLY ALIVE

Because of our sinful nature and our individual sins, we are spiritually dead and separated from God. Jesus declared, "Very truly I tell you, no one can see the kingdom of God unless they are born again" (John 3:3).

Jesus has the power to give spiritual and eternal life to all those who believe in Him and follow Him. The Gospel declares, "For since death came through a man, the resurrection of the dead comes also through a man. For as in Adam all die, so in Christ all will be made alive" (1 Corinthians 15:21–22).

As an electric lightbulb becomes full of light and useful when it is connected with electrical power, you will become full of life when you put your faith in Jesus Christ as your Savior. You will start fulfilling the purpose for which you were created.

WHAT DOES IT MEAN TO BE "BORN AGAIN"?

All you need to do is believe that Jesus died on the cross to pay the penalty for all your sins. The moment you invite Jesus to come into your life, He will enter your life through His Spirit, and you will be born again. Jesus said, "I stand at the door [of your heart] and knock. If anyone hears my voice and opens the door, I will come in" (Revelation 3:20).

To become "born again" means you are newly created in your heart and transformed in the very depths of your being. The Holy Spirit comes to dwell within you and gives you many spiritual blessings. He gives you a new heart (with new affections and desires), new power, and a new destination. You develop a new view of people around you, a new nature, and a new purpose! The Bible declares, "If anyone is in Christ, he is a new creation" (2 Corinthians 5:17 NKJV). Adam was the head of the old creation, but Christ is the head of the new creation. Certainly, you will enjoy an unimaginable inner peace, which fills your innermost being when you are "born again."

God Looks at the Heart

The Bible teaches that God is concerned about our hearts not our rituals. Jesus quoted Isaiah's prophecy: "These people [religious Jews] honor me with their lips, but their hearts are far from me. They worship me in vain; their teachings are merely human rules" (Matthew 15:8–9).

Consider an example of two men attempting to get close

to God. One man performs all the rituals he learned from his religious teachers. He memorizes and utters all the prescribed prayers, bows down with proper body movements, and washes his body for cleansing. However, he is keeping a sin in his heart. The other man was never taught the prescribed rituals and prayers, but he recognizes his sins and humbly asks God with all his heart to forgive him and guide him. According to the Bible, God would surely hear and answer the prayer of the second man.

According to the Bible, repentance (*toba* in Arabic) is making a decision and commitment to forsake all sins and to submit to God's will. Repentance involves humbling self, confessing unworthiness, and receiving God's mercy and grace that came to us through Jesus.

The wonderful truth is that if you believe in what Jesus Christ (AL-Masih Isa) did for you on the cross, and you confess your sins and repent, you will be born again! After your new birth, you will begin to enjoy a peaceful, personal, and living relationship with your Creator!

My dear reader, God wants you to take a step of faith and decide in your heart and declare with your mouth to God that you believe and rely on Jesus' death on the cross to pay the penalty for your sins.

The decision is as simple as trusting a chair to hold your weight when you sit upon it. When you put your faith in Jesus for the forgiveness of your sin—not in yourself or your works or anything else—you will experience God's forgiveness and enjoy amazing rest.

The Holy Spirit Dwells within the True Followers of Christ

True believers and followers of Christ are people who have experienced a new birth. Note that many people claim to be

Christians. Perhaps they have Christian parents, or received a Christian education, or were born in a supposedly Christian nation, or accept Christianity as a good religion. They might even be attending a church, or trying to do good works, or agreeing with Christian beliefs intellectually. However, none of those things can make someone a true follower of Christ (Christian). Only those people who experience the new birth become true followers of Christ. The evidence of the new birth is the presence of the Holy Spirit within, confirming a person to be God's child.

God Shows Mercy to Us through Jesus

What a loving God! He showed us mercy through Jesus Christ. Because of Jesus, we can actually trade judgment for forgiveness! We can trade our sin for the righteousness of Jesus. The Bible declares,

> As for you, you were dead in your transgressions and sins, in which you used to live when you followed the ways of this world. . . . All of us also lived among them at one time, gratifying the cravings of our flesh and following its desires and thoughts. Like the rest, we were by nature deserving of wrath. But because of his great love for us, God, who is rich in mercy, made us alive with Christ even when we were dead in transgressions. (Ephesians 2:1–5)

Even the Qur'an states that Jesus is a mercy from God. "And (we wish) to appoint him . . . a Mercy from us" (Surah 19:21).

Jesus Reconciles Us to God Forever!

The Bible reveals that God wants mankind to spend eternity enjoying joyful fellowship with Him (1 Timothy 2:3–4).

Jesus Christ offers us the opportunity to be born into His

spiritual family. Jesus is alive now. And through our union to Him, He alone grants us eternal life. Remember, eternal life was God's original intent for Adam and his descendants. Through Adam we all forfeited eternal life. Therefore, God sent Jesus, who willingly came to bring us back into an eternal relationship with God.

The Bible states, "All this is from God, who *reconciled* us to himself through Christ. . . . God was reconciling the world to himself in Christ, not counting people's sins against them" (2 Corinthians 5:18–19, italics added).

Some of my Muslim friends respond to this truth saying, "It is not fair that Jesus paid for our sins. Each one who has committed sin must account for it."

I usually answer, "This incredible sacrifice is not something we requested or forced someone else to give for us. It is what God Himself has done for us—as a gift. And God is simply asking you to accept His gift of reconciliation."

I also remind my Muslim friends that Jesus freely chose to rescue us; Jesus said: "I lay down my life. . . . No one takes it from me, but I lay it down of my own accord" (John 10:17–18).

A few times, I have seen fathers and mothers sacrificing their lives in order to save their children's lives.

I would like to share a story with you. Once there was a rich king who was also the lawgiver and supreme judge of his kingdom. One day his beloved son committed serious violations of the law. The penalty of these violations amounted to paying a fine of a large amount of money, which his son did not have. His father, the king, because he was a just judge, ordered his son to pay this fine because he did not want to violate his own laws. The son was terrified because if he did not pay this fine he would have to go to prison for a long time.

The son realized his mistakes and repented with all his heart for breaking the laws. The king decided to offer to pay the fine from his personal finances. The son humbly and joyfully accepted his father's gift. Out of his gratitude and love for his father, the son decided to dedicate the rest of his life to serve his father and his kingdom.

There are similarities between this story and our relationship with God. It is a small picture of what the God of the Bible has done for us. He personally paid the price we owed.

Imagine a door that opens into heaven and gives you access to the presence of God. There is such a door. Jesus said, "I am the gate; whoever enters through me will be saved" (John 10:9). The Bible tells us that Jesus is the key to heaven.

SOME BIBLICAL FACTS ABOUT JESUS

1. God the Father sent Jesus Christ. (John 8:29, 42)
2. Jesus always did the Father's will. (John 5:30)
3. Jesus could do nothing independently of the Father. (John 5:19)
4. Jesus lived to please the Father. (John 8:29)
5. Jesus Christ received all His authority from the Father. (John 5:27)
6. Jesus received His message from the Father. (John 14:10) Jesus said, "For I did not speak on my own, but the Father who sent me commanded me to say all that I have spoken. I know that his command leads to eternal life. So whatever I say is just what the Father has told me to say." (John 12:49–50)
7. The Father gave to Jesus Christ the works to accomplish. (John 5:36 and 17:4)
8. Jesus was submitted to the Father. (Matthew 26:39, 42)
9. Jesus Christ's kingdom was appointed to Him by the Father. (Luke 22:29)

10. Jesus Christ will ultimately deliver up the kingdom unto the Father. (1 Corinthians 15:24)
11. Jesus Christ Himself will be subjected unto the Father. (1 Corinthians 15:27–28)
12. God the Father is the God of Jesus Christ. (John 20:17) Jesus Christ bore the relation of man to God the Father.
13. Jesus Christ functioned under the Father's headship. (1 Corinthians 11:3) Jesus said, "The Father is greater than I." (John 14:28)
14. Jesus Christ served as a man. (Philippians 2:5–8)
15. Jesus Christ, as a human, was subject to hunger, thirst, agony, and death. (Matthew 21:18; John 19:28, 33–37)
16. The goal of Jesus was not to receive glory for Himself. (John 8:50) Jesus came, lived, suffered, and died to glorify God the Father.
17. Jesus' mission was to make it possible for us to have fellowship with God, the Bible tells us: "For Christ also suffered once for sins, the righteous for the unrighteous, to bring you to God." (1 Peter 3:18)

SECTION THREE

ABRAHAM IN THE QUR'AN AND IN THE BIBLE

8

THE LIFE OF ABRAHAM

braham is given the title "friend of God" in both the Qur'an and the Bible. Surah 4:125 teaches: "For Allah did take Abraham for a friend."

ABRAHAM, THE FRIEND OF GOD

In the Bible (James 2:23), Abraham is described as "God's friend." The title suggests a very close relationship with God. It implies that God shared with Abraham many of His secret plans for the future that He would not otherwise have revealed to someone who was only His servant.

The Bible also calls Abraham the "father of all who believe" (Romans 4:11). In Galatians 3:7, it is written, "Understand, then, that those who have faith are children of Abraham." The same concept is found in the Qur'an, which exhorts Muslims to "follow the religion of Abraham" (Surah 3:95).

In Surah 16:123, Muslims are directed to "follow the ways of Abraham, the true in faith."

Abraham is an example of the *true religion* and a model for Muslims. Abraham is also a model for true Christians. All true believers of the Gospel are to have the same *saving faith* Abraham had. (See Galatians 3:8–9.) Abraham was a prototype of the true religion to come, through his faith in God.

THE PROMISED SON—
ISAAC (ISHAQ) OR ISHMAEL (ISMAIL)?

God promised Abraham a son. Abraham was fully aware of the physical impossibility for him and his wife, Sarah, to have a son so late in life. She was barren. Yet Abraham believed God would fulfill His promise supernaturally.

Qur'anic References to the "Promised Son" and to Isaac

God commanded Abraham to sacrifice his son. The only reference to the sacrifice of the son of Abraham is in Surah 37:99–107, which reads, "So We gave him the good news of a boy ready to suffer and forbear. Then, when (the son) reached (the age of) (serious) work with him, he [Abraham] said: 'O my son! I see in vision that I offer thee in sacrifice.'"

Although this passage does not directly say which son it was, the Qur'an in this passage indicates that it is the same son whose birth is described as good news. Just two verses after the mention of the sacrifice, Isaac's birth is mentioned as good news: "Peace and salutation to Abraham . . . and We gave him the good news of Isaac. . . . We blessed him and Isaac" (Surah 37:109–113). Earlier, in Surah 11:71, Isaac's birth is foretold as good news: "But We gave her Glad tidings of Isaac." Angels announced Isaac's birth as good news, "And they [angels] gave him Glad tidings of a son . . . his wife came forward (laughing) aloud! She smote her forehead and said, 'A barren old woman!'" (Surah 51:28–29). Much attention is given to Isaac in the Qur'an.

It is significant that al-Tabari, the prominent Muslim-Arab historian and theologian, identifies Isaac as the boy to be sacrificed in Surah 37:101.[1]

Also, it's very important to mention that Muhammad's companions believed that the son to be sacrificed was Isaac.[2]

Limited Qur'anic References to Ishmael

The Qur'an actually contains no reference to the birth of Ishmael, and it doesn't foretell that Abraham will be the father of Ishmael. Nowhere in the Qur'an is it specifically stated that Ishmael was promised to Abraham by name—yet Isaac was. Very little is said in the Qur'an about Ishmael, and no attention is given to his mother or his sons. Ishmael's birth is never announced as good news. It is apparent that the son about whom the good news was given and the one to be sacrificed, as mentioned in Surah 37:99–107, was not Ishmael, but Isaac.

Abdullah Yusuf Ali, in his internationally acknowledged translation and commentary of the Qur'an, made a significant admission regarding Surah 37:99–107 (the only passage referring to the sacrifice of Abraham's son). Ali states, "The boy thus born was according to Muslim Traditions in the Hadith (which, however, are not unanimous on this point), the first born son of Abraham, viz., Ishmael."[3] Ali's claim that the firstborn son to be sacrificed was Ishmael is not based upon evidence from the Qur'an, but rather on Traditions, which he points out are not unanimous on this point.

Abraham's Promised Son Is Isaac

Muslims and Christians agree that Sarah was Isaac's mother and Hagar (Hajar) was Ishmael's mother. It is important to note that the Qur'an never mentions Hagar, and yet Sarah is mentioned a few times. And the Qur'an presented Sarah as Abraham's wife. We read: "And his wife was standing (there) and she laughed: But we gave her glad tidings of Isaac" (Surah 11:71).

One of the Traditions confirms that Hagar was only a servant in Abraham's household, "When Sarah gave her to Abraham to bear him a son. Then he called Hagar who was the most trustworthy of his servants, and he bestowed her (Hagar) on her (Sarah) and gave her clothes. Subsequently Sarah made a gift of her (Hagar) to Ibrahim who cohabitated with her and she bore Ismail who was the eldest of his children."[4]

It is also significant that Hagar and Ishmael left Abraham's house many years earlier, before God commanded Abraham to sacrifice his son (Genesis 21:14). Isaac was Abraham's only son by his wife Sarah, who had the right to inherit from Abraham.

The Qur'an claims that because Abraham and his son had fully submitted themselves to obey God, God blessed them. We read first about Abraham and Isaac, "They had both submitted their wills (to Allah)" (Surah 37:103).

Then we read, "We blessed him and Isaac" (Surah 37:113). Clearly these two verses relate. As a result of Abraham's and Isaac's full submission to God's will, God's blessing came upon them.

The Qur'an is silent and does not identify the son that God commanded Abraham to sacrifice. One of the most famous and explicit narratives in the Jewish and Christian Scriptures is God's command to Abraham to sacrifice Isaac (Genesis 22:2; Hebrews 11:17; and James 2:21). The Qur'an claims that it was sent by God to confirm the Holy Scriptures of the Jews and the Christians (Surah 5:48). If the Qur'an had come to correct any errors, as some Muslim scholars claim, the Qur'an would clearly identify Ishmael as the promised son that God commanded Abraham to sacrifice.

Surah 37, which is the only Surah to record the story of God's command to Abraham to sacrifice his son, mentions many of the prophets by name, such as Noah, Abraham, Isaac, Moses, Aaron, Elijah, and Jonah. If Ishmael were the son to be offered as a sacrifice, why didn't this Surah even mention him among the prophets, as it recognized Isaac?

The references from the Qur'an and the evidence I mentioned strongly suggest that Isaac—not Ishmael—is the son announced by God to be sacrificed.

God Bestowed "Prophethood" on the Children of Israel

God loves the Arabs, Jews, and all people equally. He desires to have a relationship with every one of them. God promised Abraham He would bless his son, Ishmael (Ismail). God told Abraham: "And as for Ishmael, I have heard you: I will surely bless him; I will make him fruitful and will greatly increase his numbers. . . . But my covenant I will establish with Isaac, whom Sarah will bear to you" (Genesis 17:20–21).

God chose to reveal prophecy to the Jewish people. It is important to read verses in the Qur'an that confirm the biblical teaching that "prophethood" was confined to the children of Israel. For example, Surah 45:16 states, "We did aforetime grant to the children of Israel the Book, the Power of Command, and Prophethood . . . and We favored them above the nations." In this verse, "the Book" means the Holy Scriptures. "Prophethood" means the prophetic line was to come through Isaac's offspring alone.

The Qur'an's words are emphatic, and they point to the superiority of Isaac's role over Ishmael.

Surah 29:27 states, "And We gave (Abraham) Isaac and Jacob, and ordained among his progeny Prophethood and Revelation." This verse and others in the Qur'an are in full agreement with God's words in the Torah: "Then God said, 'Yes, but your wife

Sarah will bear you a son, and you will call him Isaac. I will establish my covenant with him as an everlasting covenant for his descendants after him'" (Genesis 17:19).

Also found in the Torah (in Genesis 26:4; 28:14) is God's promise to Isaac and Jacob that through their seed all the families of the earth would be blessed. That promise was fulfilled by Jesus (the Messiah), who came through their lineage.

God chose that His blessings will come though Isaac because he was born through a miracle.

The story started when God promised to give Abraham many descendants. Sarah was barren and she decided not to wait for God to fulfill His promise, and she thought the way to make that happen was by giving Hagar to Abraham to marry her. And Ishmael was born in the natural way because Hagar was young and not barren like Sarah.

However God spoke to Abraham again that he and Sarah will have a son (Genesis 17:19).

Abraham believed in God's Word and promise and Sarah became pregnant and she gave birth to a son (Isaac) for Abraham in his old age.

God chose Isaac because he came as a result of Abraham's faith in God's power and grace.

THE DIFFICULT TEST OF ABRAHAM'S FAITH

"Some time later God tested Abraham. He said to him, 'Abraham!'

'Here I am,' he replied.

Then God said, 'Take your son, your only son, whom you love—Isaac—and go to the region of Moriah. Sacrifice him there as a burnt offering on a mountain I will show you.'" (Genesis 22:1–2)

Abraham must have thought deeply about God's shocking and apparently immoral command. For God had promised Abraham that through his son Isaac he would have many descendants. His descendants were to be "as numerous as the stars in the sky and as countless as the sand on the seashore" (Hebrews 11:12; Genesis 15:5 and 32:12).

Earlier in Genesis 21:12–13, God told Abraham to send Ishmael away. And now He asked him to sacrifice Isaac. Can you imagine how Abraham must have felt? Naturally Abraham would want to cling to Isaac, because Isaac was now the only remaining son that he had.

Abraham Trusted God

Abraham no doubt wondered, "How can I have the descendants promised to me if I sacrifice my son, Isaac, as God has commanded?" Abraham believed in God's promises, His faithfulness, and His righteousness. He concluded that the only way Isaac could beget offspring—after being sacrificed—would be if God were to raise him from the dead. Abraham reasoned that since God gave him a son when it was naturally impossible to have one, then God could also raise that son back to life from the dead.

Abraham Passed the Test

The Bible makes it clear that Abraham passed this great test of faith by deciding to sacrifice Isaac. In obedience, he prepared his promised son, Isaac, to be sacrificed. "By faith Abraham, when God tested him, offered Isaac as a sacrifice. He who had embraced the promises was about to sacrifice his one and only son, even though God had said to him, 'It is through Isaac that your offspring will be reckoned.' Abraham reasoned that God could even raise the dead, and so in a manner of speaking he did receive Isaac back from death" (Hebrews 11:17–19).

The Qur'an shows harmony with Abraham's reasoning in Surah 2:260: "Behold! Abraham said: 'My Lord! Show me how Thou givest life to the dead.'"

Abraham's Profound Faith

Abraham's decision to obey God and sacrifice his son was not simply mindless or blind, uncomprehending submission to the will of God. Abraham believed that God would always be faithful to His word. He realized that the promise of descendants and blessings would be fulfilled in spite of the sacrifice of his son. Abraham believed that God would raise Isaac from the dead. For that reason Abraham knew that sacrificing his son was not in any way the same as idolaters sacrificing their children to their gods.

Abraham discovered the harmony between God's shocking and apparently immoral command and God's goodness. Abraham trusted in the holy character of God.

9

THE GOSPEL PREACHED TO AND THROUGH ABRAHAM

We see the prominence of Abraham in both the Qur'an and the Bible. The Qur'an states that God told Abraham, "I will make thee an Imam to the nations" (Surah 2:124). Pickthall's translation of this verse reads, "I have appointed thee a leader for mankind." As recorded in Genesis 22:18, God promised Abraham, "Through your offspring [seed] all nations [families] on earth will be blessed."

GOD'S COVENANT WITH ABRAHAM

God told Abraham, "As for me, this is my covenant with you: You will be the father of many nations" (Genesis 17:4). Abraham considered why he was made a blessing for mankind and the father of a multitude of nations. So Abraham saw his chosen and high status as a reflection of God's great glory in heaven.

Abraham realized that he resembled the heavenly Father as a human prototype of God Himself.

He surely also viewed Isaac's miraculous birth, expected sacrifice and resurrection from the dead, and his innumerable descendants promised as types of a greater reality yet to come.

Abraham Foresaw the Good News of a Greater Sacrifice

Abraham understood that the heavenly Father also would have a Son born miraculously into this world. The Son would be offered as a sacrifice by the hand of His own Father. The Son would rise from the dead. And the risen Son would be the source of blessings to the world.

God revealed to His friend Abraham His plan of salvation and the coming blessing to mankind. Abraham foresaw the heart of the Gospel. Jesus told the Jews, "Your father Abraham rejoiced at the thought of seeing my day; he saw it and was glad" (John 8:56). Abraham must have reasoned in his mind, "What God commanded me to do for Him cannot be more than what God is willing to do for me."

Abraham had some knowledge of the true religion to come. God revealed to His friend Abraham in some measure, that someday He would send His own Son to die for the sins of the world and that any person who trusts in God's saving grace will be blessed and be saved. Note that after centuries of animal sacrifices in the Jewish temple, John the Baptist (called the prophet Yahya in the Qur'an) came and proclaimed the arrival of Jesus. John 1:29 states, "The next day John saw Jesus coming toward him and said, 'Look, the Lamb of God, who takes away the sin of the world!'"

It is amazing and significant to find the Christian message, indeed the heart of the Gospel, written all over the Jewish Holy Scripture!

The Righteousness of Abraham Resulted from His Faith

In spite of Abraham's sins, which are recorded in the Bible and in the Qur'an (Surah 26:82), God forgave Abraham and declared him to be righteous. Abraham's faith in God, and in His ability to perform what He had promised, was accepted by God as righteousness. Genesis 15:6 states, "Abram [Abraham] believed the LORD, and the LORD counted him as righteous because of his faith" (NLT).

Abraham's faith was an awesome example because he did not simply or merely bow to God's command but Abraham believed that God's command was consistent with God's faithfulness. Abraham depended on the righteousness, goodness, and trustworthiness of God. Thus his faith gave glory to God. Abraham's righteousness was not earned but a God-given righteousness.

Abraham's righteous status before God did not come from his own piety or merit earned by accumulating enough good works. Neither did it result from genetic lineage. God accepted Abraham as righteous because of his belief in God and faith in His power, His grace, and His faithfulness. The "faith" principle is explained in the Bible:

> Yet he [Abraham] did not waver through unbelief regarding the promise of God, but was strengthened in his faith and gave glory to God, being fully persuaded that God had power to do what he had promised. This is why "it was credited to him as righteousness." The words "it was credited to him" were written not for him alone, but also for us, to whom God will credit righteousness—for us who believe in him who raised Jesus our Lord from the dead. He was delivered over to death for our sins and was raised to life for our justification. (Romans 4:20–25)

Who Are the True Children of Abraham?

The true children of Abraham are those who have his faith, regardless of race or ancestry. The Bible makes this reality clear:

Consider Abraham: he

"believed God, and it was credited to him as righteousness."

Understand, then, that those who *have faith* are children of Abraham. Scripture foresaw that God would justify the Gentiles [non Jews] *by faith*, and announced the gospel in advance to Abraham: "All nations will be blessed through you." So those who rely on faith are blessed along with Abraham, the man of faith. (Galatians 3:6–9, italics added)

Verses 13 and 14 further clarify that our identification with Abraham is based on faith. "Christ redeemed us . . . in order that the blessing given to Abraham might come to the Gentiles through Christ Jesus, so that by faith we might receive the promise of the [Holy] Spirit." In other words, just as Abraham was saved by faith, the real children of Abraham are those who have faith in God and His promises. They are not those who rely on their own ability to keep the laws of God.

Everyone who has this faith receives the blessing of justification. "Therefore, the promise comes by faith, so that it may be by grace and may be guaranteed to all Abraham's offspring" (Romans 4:16).

The Messiah Came through Abraham's Lineage

God promised Abraham "through your offspring [seed] all nations on earth will be blessed" (Genesis 22:18). Jesus is called the son of Abraham in Matthew 1:1. The New Testament clarifies that Jesus is this seed of Abraham. "The promises were spoken to Abraham and to his seed. Scripture does not say, 'and to seeds,' meaning many people, but 'and to your seed,' meaning one person, who is Christ" (Galatians 3:16).

The Bible clearly tells us that Jesus, the Messiah, descended from Abraham and came to earth to accomplish our salvation. Jesus' coming and sacrifice fulfilled God's promise to Abraham of the blessing to all people. By believing in Jesus, as Abraham did, people from all nations can receive salvation and be blessed with everlasting life!

Reconciliation Is Possible

Through faith in Jesus, the children of Ishmael and the children of Isaac can have a peaceful relationship with each other as part of God's blessing to all people. I believe God wants them to be united in one happy family to enjoy peace, love, joy, and laughter.

GOD'S SACRIFICIAL LOVE FOR US

Have you ever wondered why God asked the father Abraham to give Him his son instead of asking him to fast and pray or give him anything else?

God did not ask Abraham to give Him his land or possessions, but God asked him to give Him his son because a man's own son is more precious to his heart than anything else.

And I am sure that you will agree with me, my Muslim friend, that because Abraham was willing to give up his own son to God, he proved that he was willing to give God anything and everything he had.

And that is exactly what God wants you to discover about Him. We read about God in the Bible: "He who did not spare his own Son, but gave him up for us all—how will he not also, along with him, graciously give us all things?" (Romans 8:32).

Let me give you a real example: my wife, Hala, and I prayed that someone would donate a building or a house to our ministry. Let us assume that happens, and then we need a chair to put in this building. I am sure I can ask this person to get us a chair, and he will because he gave us a building.

My Muslim friend, I strongly encourage you now to repent and put your faith in Jesus that He died to pay the penalty for your sins, so you can begin living your life knowing for sure that God will give you everything good throughout your life here on earth and forever.

Abraham had to make a choice between his love for God and his love for his son. Abraham's willingness to sacrifice his son to God proved that he loved God more than his son and more than anything else in life.

When God commanded Abraham to sacrifice his son, Abraham no doubt suffered deeply as a father. He was ripped at the depth of his being as he took his living son (who came from him) to sacrifice him with his own hand.

My Muslim friend, I am sure you will agree with me that when Abraham obeyed God and was ready to sacrifice his son to God, he proved beyond any doubt that he had perfect sacrificial love toward God. And God wants you to discover that He proved His perfect awesome love toward you in the same way, as we read in the Bible: "God demonstrates his own love for us in this: while we were still sinners, Christ died for us" (Romans 5:8).

Please, allow me to ask an important question: Has God in Islam ever matched Abraham's supreme example of love?

Has the Qur'an revealed the perfect sacrificial love of God toward you and me?

The significant question here is, can a man's love for God, such as Abraham's, surpass God's love for man?

The logical answer is, God never asked any man, including

Abraham, to do more for Him than He was willing to do.

Abraham must have reasoned that what God commanded him to do was no more than what God was willing to do for him.

God bestowed on us the greatest form of love by giving His own Son, who was not created and whose presence He enjoyed from all eternity.

God sacrificed what was most precious to His heart. The Bible shows us that God's love for Abraham and for us far surpasses Abraham's love for God.

Leading with Sacrificial Love

I have read some true stories of World War II battles that illustrate different types of leaders. One of the military commanders leading a British unit ordered his troops to advance into the battlefield. While his soldiers were being wounded and killed, his cold heart kept him far from the action.

Another military commander, whose name was James, leading a different British unit, saw that his soldiers were surrounded by the enemy. He ordered them to engage in warfare, and he joined them on the front lines. He was able to lead them to victory against all odds, and he saved the lives of most of his soldiers. However, he himself was cut down. This leader laid down his life for his men.

The second leader shows us a glimpse of how God has led His people to victory, even giving of Himself for their sake. God's love is perfect. The true test and measure of love is sacrifice. Jesus said, "Greater love has no one than this: to lay down one's life for one's friends" (John 15:13).

When you look at the cross, at Jesus who hung upon it, you see the depth and intensity of God's infinite and eternal love for you.

Jesus is God's most precious gift to you. Would you receive His gift by opening your heart to Jesus by faith right now? Faith is the response God seeks to find in you.

10

GOD RANSOMED ABRAHAM'S SON

The Qur'an tells us that God had commanded Abraham to sacrifice his son, and as he was about to perform this sacrifice, God intervened. "... *Ibrāhïm* said to him: 'O my son! I have seen a vision that I should offer you as a sacrifice ...'.... And when they both submitted to Allah and *Ibrāhïm* laid down his son prostrate upon his forehead for sacrifice; We called out to him: 'O Ibrāhïm [Abraham] stop! You have fulfilled your vision.' Thus do We reward the righteous. That was indeed a manifest test. We ransomed his son for a great sacrifice ..." (Surah 37:101–107, Muhammad Farooq-I-Azam Malik).

GOD PROVIDED A SUBSTITUTE SACRIFICE

In the story of Abraham recorded in the Qur'an, Surah 37, Abraham was about to sacrifice his son but God stopped him and set the son free. Did God simply allow the prophet Abraham to take his son and leave? No, a sacrificial offering was still required.

The only way God chose to free Abraham's son was by substituting another sacrifice. The principle of redemption is stated clearly in this story, for a ram was slain to redeem Abraham's son.

God loved Abraham's son, and, therefore, He rescued (ransomed) him. God provided a ram to be offered in his place (Genesis 22:13). Note that it was God who provided the alternate sacrifice.

Likewise, my Muslim friend, it was God who ransomed us by a sacrifice that He Himself provided. And His motive was His love for us!

A "Momentous," "Mighty," and "Tremendous" Sacrifice

We read in the Gospel that when John the Baptist saw Jesus coming toward him, John proclaimed, "Look, the Lamb of God, who takes away the sin of the world!" (John 1:29). The Lamb of God is Jesus (AL-Masih Isa).

The prophet Isaiah, inspired of God, prophesied about the coming Messiah and recognized Him to be the sacrificial lamb: "He was oppressed and afflicted, yet he did not open his mouth; he was led like a lamb to the slaughter, and as a sheep before its shearers is silent, so he did not open his mouth" (Isaiah 53:7).

Abdullah Yusuf Ali translation of Surah 37:107 states: "We ransomed him with a momentous sacrifice." Other universally recognized translators of the same Surah described the sacrifice as "tremendous" and "mighty."

The Sacrificed Ram Represented a Much Greater Truth

The logical question is: What kind of sacrifice deserves to be called "momentous," "mighty," and "tremendous"? Obviously the animal (ram) that God provided for Abraham was not intended to fit this description. It was only a symbol of the greater sacrifice to come—Jesus Christ.

The answer is clearly stated in the Bible, "For you know that it was not with perishable things . . . that you were redeemed[1] from the empty way of life handed down to you from your ancestors, but with the precious blood of Christ, a lamb without blemish or defect" (1 Peter 1:18–19).

Biblical scholar D. C. Halverson poses a thought-provoking question: "If salvation is only a matter of rewarding those who do good, and if God's purpose was only to test Abraham's obedience, why then was there a need for a 'momentous sacrifice'? Was it not sufficient that Abraham went as far as he did (by obeying God's command)?"[2]

GOD'S GIFT OF GRACE CAME TO US THROUGH JESUS

The Gospel tells us that because God loves us so much, He rescued us through the ultimate sacrifice of Jesus. The Qur'an describes AL-Masih Isa (Jesus) as "a Spirit proceeding from God" (Surah 4:171). Jesus took our place and was sacrificed on our behalf. He died on the cross as a ransom to free us from the penalty owed for our sins. Jesus said, "The Son of Man did not come to be served, but to serve, and to give his life as a ransom for many" (Matthew 20:28).

The most valuable sacrifice God could give us was of Himself. For this reason He came to our world in the person of Jesus to save us. The Lamb's sacrifice is "exceedingly wonderful" because it represents God's sacrifice of Himself, which is of infinite value and sufficient for our salvation!

Please allow me to illustrate this ultimate act of love through another story. One day, a young man committed a murder. The police chased after him on the ground and in the air, but he managed to get home to his family.

His father was shocked to see that his son's clothing was

stained with blood. The son confessed to his father that he just killed someone and that the police sirens and the helicopter overhead were for him. The father told his son to take off his clothes quickly. The father put on his son's clothing and gave his clean clothes to his son and asked him to wear them. The police pounded on the door of the house and barged in. When they saw the father's clothes stained with blood, they arrested him. The father paid for his son's crime. Jesus said, "Greater love has no one than this, than to lay down one's life for his friends" (John 15:13 NKJV).

WHO COULD PROVIDE THE PRICE FOR OUR RANSOM?

In Surah 10:54, we read: "Every soul that hath sinned, if it possessed all that is on earth, would fain give it in ransom." A "ransom" is defined as the required price to pay for the release of a captive.[3] God was the only One able to provide a ransom for our freedom from spiritual death and punishment.

In the Torah (Leviticus 4), God commanded the people to sacrifice an innocent animal, such as a lamb, a sheep, or a goat that had no flaw or blemish, to cover their sins. The animal was brought to the priest, and the sinner would lay his hands on the animal's head (as a sign of identification) and confess his sins. And so the sins were transferred onto the animal and its throat was slit. Then the priest would spread the animal's blood upon the altar for the remission of sins. Thus the penalty for sin was paid for by the innocent animal's death as a substitute for the sinful person.

It is true that the clean, innocent animal was not guilty of any crime, but God desired to show the people how serious sin is in His eyes. The Old Testament (Covenant) presented the foundation for the teachings of the Gospel.

The Bible declares, "Just think how much more the blood of Christ will purify our consciences from sinful deeds so that we can worship the living God. For by the power of the eternal Spirit, Christ offered himself to God as a perfect sacrifice for our sins. That is why he is the one who mediates a new covenant between God and people, so that all who are called can receive the eternal inheritance God has promised them. For Christ died to set them free from the penalty of the sins they had committed under that first covenant" (Hebrews 9:14–15 NLT).

Do you see the significance of the cross, my dear Muslim friend? Christ sacrificed His life in order to give us the right to live forever, freeing us from the debt we owe—the penalty for our sins. Jesus was our substitute. He paid the price for us.

Biblical scholar John Stott expressed the heart of the Gospel by saying: "Divine love triumphed over divine wrath by divine self-sacrifice."

Jesus said, "This is my blood of the covenant, which is poured out for many for the forgiveness of sins" (Matthew 26:28).

When Jesus said "my blood . . . is poured out for many," He meant His life would be given for many. Jesus' death inaugurated the new relationship (which is called covenant or testament) between God and His people. This covenant would replace the old Mosaic covenant, which Moses sealed between God and the people by sprinkling the altar with the blood of animals (Exodus 24:6).

Significance of Blood Sacrifice in Islam

It is interesting to read in the Qur'an that Moses said to his people that God is commanding you to sacrifice a sound and unblemished heifer (Surah 2:67–71).

According to Muhammad (as recorded in Al-Bukhari), animal sacrifice was an acknowledged, divinely appointed means of gaining God's acceptance.[4] Muslims celebrate an annual feast called "Feast of Sacrifice" (Id Al-Adha). On this day, animals are sacrificed. The Muslim world generally believes that this festival commemorates the willingness of Abraham to offer his son as a sacrifice to God.

An Illustration of God's Ransom for Us

I am reminded of a story I read about Shamuel, a noble prince. He was trying to protect his people and land from being invaded by an evil neighboring kingdom. One night, he planned a surprise attack. But the enemy knew and was waiting for Shamuel's army to come because his secret plans had been revealed to the enemy. Many of his soldiers lost their lives, and ultimately he lost the battle. Shamuel announced that the traitor would be punished—whipped with one hundred lashes.

In great secrecy, Shamuel's army launched another attack, but again his enemy was waiting to ambush his soldiers. The prince lost another battle, but this time he discovered the traitor. It was Shamuel's own mother! She was having a romantic relationship with one of the enemy's soldiers.

What a dilemma! What should Shamuel do? If he exempted his mother from punishment, his followers would correctly accuse him of being unjust and not caring about his people. The alternative would be even more difficult for Shamuel. Because he loved his mother, how could he mandate a just sentence that would result in the suffering and most likely the death of his beloved mother?

Shamuel addressed his people, "We have lost two battles because of treason. Many of our men have been killed. The law has been broken and punishment shall be executed—*one hundred lashes*! Righteousness and justice must be maintained."

The prince's mother was filled with great fear as she was led away to the circle where she would receive her punishment. The executioner lifted his whip. But before the first blow was delivered, Shamuel shouted out, "Wait! Wait! I will take the punishment instead of her." He removed his royal clothes and commanded, "Executioner, you dare not strike me with less force than you would have used on the traitor. I am the person who will take her punishment. Do your duty—strike on!"

Lash after lash struck the back of Shamuel until he collapsed to the ground unconscious. He did, however, survive the lashings contrary to all expectations. Prince Shamuel paid in full the penalty for his beloved mother's offense in order to set her free!

Likewise, Jesus came to pay a debt He did not owe because we owed a debt we could not pay. God's Word says, "He [Jesus] personally carried our sins in his body on the cross so that we can be dead to sin and live for what is right. By his wounds you are healed" (1 Peter 2:24 NLT). Again, Jesus Himself taught, "Greater love has no one than this, that he lay down his life for his friends" (John 15:13 NKJV).

My precious Muslim reader, if you were to ask God, "How much do You love me?" He would point to Jesus, who hung on the cross with outstretched arms, and say, "I love you this much."

Jesus Means "Savior"

The well-known Muslim scholar Al-Qasemi, in his famous commentary *Mahasen at-Ta'aweel*, commented on Surah 3:45. He wrote, "The name Isa [Jesus] is an Arabic form from a Greek word, which means *Savior*."[5] Note that the Gospel, in Matthew 1:21, states, "She [Mary] will give birth to a son, and you [Joseph] are to give him the name Jesus, because he will save his people from their sins."

SECTION FOUR

JESUS IN THE QUR'AN
AND IN THE BIBLE

11

CHRIST JESUS (*AL-MASIH, ISA*) GOD'S ANOINTED MESSIAH

The Qur'an gives Jesus three distinguished titles: "Christ Jesus [*AL-Masih, Isa*], the son of Mary was . . . a messenger of Allah, His Word [*Kalimatuhuu*] . . . and a Spirit proceeding from Him [Ruhun Minhu]" (Surah 4:171).

JESUS IS THE MESSIAH IN THE QUR'AN AND THE HADITH

Jesus alone is referred to as AL-Masih (*the Messiah*) in the Qur'an. Its use of the definite article *the* positively distinguishes Jesus from all other prophets. Occasionally He is referred to solely by this title without using His name (as in Surah 4:172). Jesus is given the title the Messiah more than ten times in the Qur'an. For example, Surah 3:45 states that the angel Gabriel appeared to Mary and said the name of her son was to be "Christ Jesus" (AL-Masih, Isa, which is the Messiah, Jesus).

Jesus is called AL-Masih in the Hadith. Muslim scholars acknowledge that the title AL-Masih is not derived from an Arabic root. Scholar Al-Baidawi, commenting on Surah 3:45, says that the word *Christ* (AL-Masih) was originally a Hebrew word (*Mashih*). Note that the Qur'an does not explain the meaning of the title Messiah. By not giving an explanation of this title it implicitly agrees with what is written about the Messiah in the Bible.

The Gospel was written in the Greek language. The Greek word for AL-Masih or "The Anointed One" is *ho Christos*, from which comes the English word *Christ*. Therefore, whenever the word *Christ* is used in the English translation of the New Testament, it is the same as AL-Masih. Muslim scholars agree on this point.

BIBLE PROPHECIES OF THE COMING MESSIAH

The Old Testament was written hundreds of years before Christ came to earth. It contains many inspired prophecies of One Glorious Savior, who would one day be sent by God and would be called "Anointed One" (The Messiah) (Daniel 9:25).

There are sixty-one major prophecies in the Old Testament about the coming Messiah, which were fulfilled in Jesus with 100 percent accuracy! Many books have been written on this subject. An outstanding reference book on Messianic prophecies is *All the Messianic Prophecies of the Bible*, by Herbert Lockyer.[1]

Consider the following examples:

• **His place of birth**
Jesus was born in Bethlehem, which was foretold by the prophet Micah about seven hundred years before the coming of Christ (BC) (Micah 5:2). The historical fulfillment of this prophecy is found in Matthew 2:1, 6 and John 7:42.

◆ His virgin birth

Jesus was born of a virgin as prophesied by the prophet Isaiah seven centuries earlier, "Therefore the Lord himself will give you a sign: The virgin will conceive and give birth to a son, and will call him Immanuel" (Isaiah 7:14). We see the historical fulfillment of this prophecy in the New Testament.

"All this took place to fulfill what the Lord had said through the prophet: 'The virgin will conceive and give birth to a son, and they will call him Immanuel' (which means 'God with us')." (Matthew 1:22–23)

◆ His death by crucifixion

Psalm 22 describes death on the cross. David (Daud) wrote about the crucifixion one thousand years before the coming of Christ. Verse 16 states, "Dogs surround me, a pack of villains encircles me; they pierce my hands and my feet."

The "piercing" of Jesus is also prophesied in Zechariah 12:10 and later fulfilled as written in John 19:34.

◆ His betrayal

Psalm 41:9 foretold that the Messiah would be betrayed by a friend.

The New Testament fulfillment is recorded in Matthew 26:47–50 (which is when Jesus is betrayed by Judas and arrested).

◆ His mission on earth

Isaiah prophesied seven hundred years before Jesus was born: "But he was pierced for our transgressions, he was crushed for our iniquities; the punishment that brought us peace was on him, and by his wounds we are healed. We all, like sheep, have gone astray, each of us has turned to our own way; and the LORD has laid on him the iniquity of us all" (Isaiah 53:5–6).

The Bible clearly declares that the predicted Messiah is a divine person. In one of the prophecies, the coming Messiah is given divine names: "For to us a child is born, to us a son is given. . . . And he will be called Wonderful Counselor, Mighty God, Everlasting Father, Prince of Peace" (Isaiah 9:6).

The phrase "Everlasting Father" means that this child to be born is eternal and will have the heart of the perfect Father toward His people.

The prophet Isaiah foretold that the coming Messiah would be called *Immanuel*, which is a Hebrew name meaning "God with us." As written in Isaiah 7:14: "The Lord himself will give you a sign: The virgin will conceive and give birth to a son, and will call him Immanuel." The fulfillment of this prophecy is recorded in Matthew 1:21–23.

Jesus Is the Son of God and the Son of Man

Jesus called Himself "the Son of God." He said, "All things have been committed to me by my Father. No one knows the Son except the Father, and no one knows the Father except the Son" (Matthew 11:27). See also Matthew 26:63–64.

Jesus also called Himself "the Son of Man." He used these titles to make evident His humanity as well as His deity, which indicates that He is the Messiah.

The prophet Daniel used the Messianic title "Son of Man" and prophesied that the coming Messiah is divine:

"In my vision at night I looked, and there before me was one like a son of man, coming with the clouds of heaven. He approached the Ancient of Days and was led into his presence. He was given authority, glory and sovereign power; all nations and peoples of every language worshiped him. His dominion is an everlasting dominion that will not pass away, and his kingdom is one that will never be destroyed." (Daniel 7:13–14)

In this passage Daniel saw in a vision a person like a Son of Man, referring to the fact that He was human in His appearance. He also saw that this person was given sovereign power and would be worshiped by all. His dominion is everlasting and He is the king of an eternal kingdom. Obviously, this One who is like a Son of Man was more than just a man! Clearly the prophets declared in the Holy Scriptures that the coming Messiah would be far superior to a mere prophet. Both Old and New Testament Scriptures teach the divine-human nature of the Messiah (Christ).

Our Savior Jesus Christ used the term "Son of Man" on several occasions where He actually was confirming His deity. For example, Jesus said that the Son of Man has power on earth to forgive sins (Matthew 9:6). Also, Jesus said that the Son of Man is the One who shall judge the world. "For the Son of Man will come in the glory of His Father with His angels, and then He will reward each according to his works" (Matthew 16:27 NKJV). (Please see also John 3:13; Matthew 12:8; 26:63–65.)

So, the term "Son of Man" does not indicate the human nature alone nor the divine nature alone, but indicates the unity of the two natures.

Jesus Claimed to Be the Messiah

In Luke 24:44–48, Jesus said:

"This is what I told you while I was still with you: Everything must be fulfilled that is written about me [prophesied] in the Law of Moses, the Prophets and the Psalms."

Then he opened their minds so they could understand the Scriptures. He told them, "This is what is written: The Messiah will suffer and rise from the dead on the third day, and repentance for the forgiveness of sins will be preached in his name to all nations, beginning at Jerusalem. You are witnesses of these things."

In this passage, Jesus Christ confirmed God's revelation in the Old Testament to be authentic. He prepared His disciples for His future suffering and crucifixion. He told them about His resurrection.

The Jews who were there gathered around him, saying, "How long will you keep us in suspense? If you are the Messiah, tell us plainly."

Jesus answered, "I did tell you, but you do not believe. The works I do in my Father's name testify about me, but you do not believe because you are not my sheep." (John 10:24–26)

Most of the Jewish people in Jesus' day rejected Him (John 1:11).

The Messiah Came for All People and All Races

Unfortunately, in Jesus' time, many of the Jews thought the promises of God were only for them. They were incorrect. God declared in the Gospel that *all believers* are one in Christ. Faith in Christ transcends people's differences. The Bible assures us in Galatians 3:26–28 (NKJV), "You are all sons of God through faith in Christ Jesus. . . . There is neither Jew nor Greek, there is neither slave nor free, there is neither male nor female; for you [believers] are all one in Christ Jesus." (Also see Romans 3:29–30.)

The Jewish religious leaders were mistaken when they expected the coming Messiah to elevate their nation. They were also mistaken when they believed the Messiah would establish Himself as an *earthly* king. Jesus declared, "My kingdom is not of this world" (John 18:36).

We read in the Bible that Jesus asked some Jewish leaders:

"What do you think about the Messiah? Whose son is he?" They replied, "He is the son of David." Jesus responded, "Then why does David, speaking under the inspiration of the Spirit, call the Messiah 'my Lord'? For David said, 'The LORD said to my Lord, Sit in the place of honor at my right hand until I humble your enemies beneath your feet.' Since David called the Messiah 'my Lord,' how can the Messiah be his son?" No one could answer him. And after that, no one dared to ask him any more questions. (Matthew 22:41–46 NLT)

Jesus quoted Psalm 110:1 to show that David wrote about God talking to the Messiah, and David calls Messiah "my Lord." This showed that the Messiah would not be the political ruler they imagined and dreamed of.

ANNOUNCEMENT OF THE GOOD NEWS

The prophets of the Old Testament looked forward to the appearance of the great Messiah. What a great moment in the history of humanity. The good news was announced! AL-Masih, the Savior to all people, had finally arrived. God's Word proclaims His birth as "good news." This account is recorded in the Gospel. An angel appeared to a group of shepherds in the fields of Bethlehem, and the glory of the Lord shone around them. The angel made this wonderful proclamation:

> "Do not be afraid. I bring you good news that will cause great joy for all the people. Today in the town of David a Savior has been born to you; he is the Messiah, the Lord. This will be a sign to you: You will find a baby wrapped in cloths and lying in a manger." Suddenly a great company of the heavenly host appeared with the angel, praising God and saying, "Glory to God in the highest heaven, and on earth peace to those on whom his favor rests." (Luke 2:10–14)

The Qur'an Confirms Jesus' Birth as "Glad News"

The Qur'an not only agrees with the Bible that AL-Masih (the Messiah) is Jesus, the son of Mary, but it also confirms the biblical declaration that Jesus' birth is good news. It declares in Surah 3:45, "Behold! The angel said: 'O Mary! Allah giveth thee Glad Tidings of a Word from Him: His name will be Christ Jesus the son of Mary, held in honor in this world and the hereafter and of (the company of) those Nearest to Allah.'" This glad news is for you, my Muslim friend.

Opposition to the Good News

Satan (*Shaitan* in Arabic) is working hard to prevent people from understanding Jesus' nature and mission, as it is revealed throughout the Bible. The Jewish religious teachers asked Jesus' disciples, "Why does he eat with tax collectors and sinners?"

Jesus Himself replied, "Those who are well have no need of a physician, but those who are sick. I did not come to call the righteous, but sinners, to repentance" (Mark 2:17 NKJV). Jesus came for sinners like you and me.

Jesus' Miracles Attest to His Being the Messiah

The Bible prophesied that the coming Messiah would perform specific miracles (Isaiah 35:5–6). Hundreds of years later, when Jesus came to earth, He gave sight to the blind, He gave the lame the ability to walk, and He opened deaf ears. Thus, by His miracles, Jesus established that He is the promised Messiah, the Savior of the world.

References to Jesus' Miracles in the Qur'an

The Qur'an says that the miracles performed by Jesus were "clear Signs" of God's power. These clear signs were not granted to all of the prophets. The Qur'an states in Surah 2:253, "Those Messengers we endowed with gifts, some above others: . . . To Jesus, the son of Mary, we gave clear (Signs)." Commenting on this verse, Al-Baidawi said: "God made Jesus' miracles the evidence of his preferment (above all the prophets) because they are clear signs and great miracles. Together those miracles were not performed by anyone else."[2]

According to the Qur'an, Jesus declares that He creates life, heals the blind, heals lepers, and even raises people from the dead!

Jesus Alone Displayed the Great Power of God

The Gospel tells of the great multitude of people who had come to hear Jesus and to be healed of their diseases.

He [Jesus] went down with them and stood on a level place. A large crowd of his disciples was there and a great number of people from all over Judea, from Jerusalem, and from the coastal region around Tyre and Sidon, who had come to hear him and to be healed of their diseases. Those troubled by impure spirits were cured, and the people all tried to touch him, because power was coming from him and healing them all. (Luke 6:17–19)

It is surprising, and no doubt disappointing to many Muslim scholars, that the Qur'an nowhere states that Muhammad performed any miracle or sign. In fact Surah 28:48 addresses this absence, stating, "But (now), when the Truth has come to them [the Jews] from Ourselves, They say, 'Why are not (Signs) sent to him [Muhammad], like Those which were sent to Moses?'" The Qur'an records that many people did not believe in Muhammad because he did not perform any miracles. (Also see Surah 20:133 and 29:50.)

Jesus alone possesses the great power of God, and Jesus alone is able to heal spiritually and physically all who believe in Him! Perhaps you are feeling restless because of negative circumstances in your life. Perhaps you need healing or rest. Jesus says to you, "Come to me, all you who are weary and burdened, and I will give you rest" (Matthew 11:28).

12

JESUS CHRIST, "HIS WORD" (*KALIMATUHUU*)

In the Qur'an Jesus is called "His Word" (*Kalimatuhuu*), which means The Word of God. Surah 4:171 states, "Christ Jesus the son of Mary was a messenger of Allah, and His Word."

THE QUR'AN AND THE BIBLE AGREE THAT JESUS IS THE "WORD OF GOD"

The Qur'an records that the angel said to Mary, "Allah giveth thee Glad tidings of a Word from Him: his name will be Christ Jesus the Son of Mary" (Surah 3:45). My dear reader, note that this "Word" that God gave to Mary was not a mere expression—it was the very Person of Christ Jesus.

Surah 3:39 states, "Yahya witnessing the truth of a Word from Allah." The famous Muslim scholar Al Razi comments on this verse. He explains the word of God to be Jesus (Isa).[1]

The Qur'an, in Surah 3:39, agrees with the Gospel record about John the Baptist (called the Prophet Yahya in the Qur'an) proclaiming that "The Word" (Jesus) would come from God.

According to the Bible, John the Baptist was sent by God to prepare the way and to announce the coming of Jesus Christ (John 1:23–27).

The Bible clearly gave Jesus the title "the Word of God" as stated in Revelation 19:13, "He is dressed in a robe dipped in blood, and his name is the Word of God."

In the Qur'an and in the Gospel, Jesus is the only person who is given the unique title "the Word of God." The emphasis of deity in this title is clearly visible and acceptable. The person of Jesus is the Word and the source of the Word is God Himself. Although the Qur'an gives no explanation for this title, the Bible explains it.

Jesus, the Word, Is the Full Revelation of God to All Humanity

Since Jesus is the only person who is called "the Word of God" in the Bible by God Himself and the Qur'an agrees, it is clear then that Jesus must be the One and only perfect expression of God's mind and will. The Bible declares in Colossians 1:15, "He [Jesus] is the image of the invisible God."

My dear reader, it might help to remember that your words reveal the kind of person you are. Also, the Word of God (Jesus) is the personal revelation of God to us all. To know Jesus is to know God. Jesus Himself said, "Anyone who has seen me has seen the Father" (John 14:9). Jesus not only brings the revelation and words of God to men, but He Himself *is* the very Word who came down from heaven to earth (John 1:14).

Jesus' Words Are Supernatural

It is clear throughout the Gospel that the words Jesus spoke were God's words. Note that the Qur'an acknowledges the divine effect of Jesus' words. Consider Jesus' powerful words in both the Qur'an and in the Bible.

- Jesus spoke to the leper, saying, "Be clean," and he was totally cleansed (Mark 1:40–45; see Surah 3:49).
- Jesus told the paralytic, "Your sins are forgiven," and then gave him the ability to walk (Mark 2:5).
- Jesus raised a dead girl to life when He said to her; "Little girl, get up" (Mark 5:21–43; see Surah 3:49; Surah 5:110).
- Jesus calmed the storm by saying, "Quiet! Be still!" showing authority over nature (Mark 4:35–41).

Jesus' supernatural words did what only God could do. The words of the historical Jesus healed the sick, forgave the sins of sinners, and raised the dead. The ascended Jesus still speaks such words today, for He is alive!

THE ETERNAL NATURE OF THE WORD OF GOD

When you speak, my dear reader, your word comes out from you, but this same word is still in you. The Word of God, Jesus, comes out from God, yet He still exists in God. Jesus said, "I am in the Father, and . . . the Father is in me" (John 14:10). Jesus also said, "I and the Father are one" (John 10:30).

"The Word" Has Always Existed

Which came first, God or His Word? Clearly God's Word is included in His essence. No one can separate God from His Word.

The Gospel sheds more light on the title "the Word" given to Jesus in both the Qur'an and the Bible.

In the beginning the Word already existed. The Word was with God, and the Word was God. He existed in the beginning with God. God created everything through him, and nothing was created except through him. (John 1:1–3 NLT)

In these verses, the Bible specifies that in the beginning before Creation the Word already existed. Jesus has been the Word of God throughout all eternity. The Word's very nature is of God, which shows that Jesus is divine.

The Eternal Word Became Human

Jesus alone is the Word of God who came to earth in human form. The Word of God became the man Christ Jesus, the son of Mary. John 1:14 reveals, "So the Word became human and made his home among us. He was full of unfailing love and faithfulness. And we have seen his glory, the glory of the Father's one and only Son" (NLT).

The Word becoming human does not mean that the "Word" (*Logos*) ceased to be what He was. The verb "became" (*egeneto*) in this verse certainly does not mean the Logos changed into human, thus altering His essential nature. It means that He acquired an additional form (a human form) without changing His essential nature in any way.

God Communicates to Us through His Eternal Word

We have in Jesus the fullest possible expression of God toward man. It is through the Word, Jesus, that God expresses His character and communicates with us directly.

My dear reader, let me ask you, if a person you love in your family got sick, what would be your best way to communicate with him, to write him a letter or go visit him personally? The Bible clearly declares that God chose to use the most humble and loving method to communicate with us, by coming to us in the person of Jesus Christ.

An eminent Muslim scholar, Dr. Qaradawi, wrote of God's nature, "If our hearing is through the sense of hearing that gets transmitted by air, God's hearing differs from ours. And if our sight comprehends things through the sense of seeing, and the rays (of light), God's seeing is not like ours."[2] God's Word is totally different than anything else we know.

IS THE WORD OF GOD CREATED OR UNCREATED?

Al-Baidawi, one of the most famous Muslim scholars, commented on Surah 3:39: "Jesus is called the Word of God because he is like the Book of God."[3] Prominent scholar Ibn Hazm reports the leading scholar Ibn Hanbal as saying, "The Word of God is His eternal knowledge and hence it is uncreated."[4]

One of the early leaders of the Muslim world, Caliph Ma'moun (AD 786–833), significantly stated in a letter to the governor of Baghdad, that those who believe that the Qur'an is uncreated are "like Christians when they claim that Jesus the Son of Mary was not created because he was the Word of God."[5]

GOD CAME IN PERSON
AND SENT WRITTEN INSTRUCTIONS

My dear Muslim friend, I pray you will see that God, motivated by His strong love for spiritually sick mankind, was not satisfied to send only a Book. He also chose to be our personal Physician and Savior in the person of Jesus.

Imagine someone who is about to drown in the deep ocean. He can barely keep his head above the water. If you were that person, which would be your most urgent need? Someone to throw you a book of swimming instructions and ask you to try hard? Or someone to dive in the water and rescue you? In the Gospel, God tells us that the human race is sinking in the depth of sin and He personally came to rescue us!

13

JESUS CHRIST, "A SPIRIT FROM GOD" (*RUHUN MINHU*)

Surah 4:171 states, "Christ Jesus the son of Mary was a Messenger of Allah . . . and a Spirit proceeding from Him (Ruhun Minhu)." In many other well-accepted translations of the Qur'an, the term *Ruhun Minhu* is translated as "a Spirit from God."

ACCORDING TO THE QUR'AN, JESUS IS "SPIRIT FROM GOD"

In the Qur'an, Jesus, the Messiah, son of Mary, is the only one given the title "Spirit from God." Notice the Qur'an describes Jesus as a Spirit from God and not just a prophet. It is clear, however, that this title supports that Jesus was not a creature made from dust, but was an eternal Spirit who took on human flesh.

This statement affirms the preexistence of Jesus before His miraculous conception on earth. In the Islamic Traditions

(Hadith), which are a record of the words and deeds of Muhammad, Jesus is referred to as the "Spirit of God."

According to True Islam, Jesus Is God's Spirit

Al-Ahadith Al-Qudsiyyah (the highest revered group of Hadiths) stated, *"Jesus (is) the servant of Allah, His Apostle, His Word and His Spirit."*[1] In the introduction, the author highlights the divine authority of Al-Ahadith Al-Qudsiyyah as follows: "Hadith Qudsi, however, is a report of what God said, though not necessarily in His words. The divine authority, explicitly stated or implicit in the context of the Hadith Qudsi, gives this group of Hadiths a special character and significance to Muslims and non-Muslims alike."[2]

The "Spirit from God" Is Eternal

Abdullah Yusuf Ali defines the term "Spirit from God" in his internationally acclaimed translation and commentary, *The Meaning of the Holy Qur'an*. He comments on Surah 58:22, which states that God strengthens true believers with "a Spirit from Himself." In explaining what *Spirit from God* means, Ali says it is *"the Divine Spirit, which we can no more define adequately than we can define in human language the nature and attributes of Allah."*[3] This is an amazing comment because it clearly and strongly indicates that the Spirit from God is the very Spirit of the living God—uncreated and eternal.

JESUS IS ETERNAL

The words Abdullah Yusuf Ali used in his commentary are not vague. He interprets a "Spirit from God" to mean from the realm of deity and not from the created order. "Spirit from God" is the very title that the Qur'an gives to Jesus in Surah 4:171.

According to Abdullah Yusuf Ali's interpretation of the term "Spirit from God" in Surah 58:22, we can conclude that Jesus is the *eternal* divine Spirit who appeared in human flesh. My dear Muslim friend, the Qur'an calls Jesus the *Ruhun-Minhu*, which in English means "Spirit from God."

My precious reader, you are far from where God is. You can't find the way to God's presence by yourself. You need a living person who came from heaven and knows the way to heaven. This person is Jesus. Jesus said, "I am the way and the truth and the life. No one comes to the Father except through me" (John 14:6).

Jesus said to His disciples, "The Father himself loves you because you have loved me and have believed that I came from God. I came from the Father and entered the world; now I am leaving the world and going back to the Father" (John 16:27–28).

John the Baptist (Yahya) said: "The one who comes from above is above all; the one who is from the earth belongs to the earth, and speaks as one from the earth. The one who comes from heaven is above all" (John 3:31).

We believe that Jesus is united to God in One Spirit from all eternity. He took an additional nature, a human nature, and came to earth as God's ambassador. He was subject to God's authority and dwelt among us. He had two natures, one divine and one human, united in one man.

THE UNIQUE
FEATURES OF JESUS

14

THE VIRGIN BIRTH OF JESUS CHRIST

As we investigate the uniqueness of Jesus Christ in the Qur'an and in the Bible, let us do this with the confidence that God guides us as sincere seekers of truth.

THE VIRGIN BIRTH ACCORDING TO BOTH THE QUR'AN AND THE BIBLE

Jesus' miraculous conception is taught in the Qur'an. We read in Surah 19:16–22:

> And make mention of Mary in the Scripture. . . . We sent unto her Our Spirit and it assumed for her the likeness of a perfect man.
>
> She said: Lo! I seek refuge in the Beneficent One from thee. . . . He said: I am only a messenger of thy Lord, that I may bestow on thee a faultless son.

She said: how can I have a son when no mortal hath touched me, neither have I been unchaste?

He said: So (it will be). Thy Lord saith: It is easy for Me. And (it will be) that We may make of him a revelation for mankind and a mercy from Us, and it is a thing ordained.

And she conceived him . . . (Pickthall)

Jesus Was Born of the Virgin Mary

The Qur'an teaches that Jesus was conceived of a woman only. His mother was the "virgin Mary." The virgin birth of Jesus is also recorded in Surah 3:45–47. It is an amazing fact that Jesus' miraculous conception is taught in the Qur'an. Surah 21:91 clearly states: "And (remember) her who guarded her chastity. We breathed into her of Our Spirit and we made her and her son a Sign for all peoples."

According to the Gospel, Jesus was not conceived by human means, but by the power of the Holy Spirit of God. "Mary . . . was found to be pregnant through the Holy Spirit" (Matthew 1:18). (See also Luke 1:26–36.) Both the Bible and the Qur'an teach as a fact that Jesus was born of a virgin woman by the will of God through the power of the Spirit of God. Jesus was the only Man in all creation who was born in this unique, divine way. Many Muslims, during my conversation with them, tell me: "Adam's life was more unique than Jesus' because he came without a father and without a mother." I usually smile and remind my Muslim friends that Adam could not have had a father or a mother because Adam was the first man God created on earth.

Jesus' Supernatural Birth Was a Sign to All Men

It is remarkable that in the Qur'an only the birth of Jesus is said to be a *sign* for everyone! It states twice that Christ's supernatural birth took place by God's purpose to give men a sign.

Surah 21:91 states, "We made her and her son a Sign for all people." In Surah 19:21, we read: " (We wish) to appoint him as a Sign unto men and a Mercy from us . . ."

It is also significant to find that Jesus' mother is the only woman mentioned by name in the entire Qur'an. Surah 19 is named *Maryam* (Mary). In fact, Mary's name appears many times in the Qur'an while Eve, the first woman God created, is nowhere mentioned by name.

Mary Was Honored above All Women

Both the Qur'an and the Bible teach that Mary is the most honored woman in the history of mankind. Surah 3:42 declares, "Behold! The angels said: 'O Mary! Allah hath chosen thee . . . above the women of all nations.'" And in Luke 1:42, Mary receives a prophecy: "Blessed are you among women, and blessed is the child you will bear!"

One must wonder why Mary is honored above all women ever. The reason is clear. It is because God chose Mary to be the mother of the only perfect and divine Man who ever lived on the face of the earth!

Even Muhammad stated that Jesus' birth was the only birth in which Satan could not interfere.[1] My dear Muslim friend, are you beginning to see the uniqueness of Jesus?

THE REASON FOR THE VIRGIN BIRTH

The Gospel teaches that Jesus is the divine Son of God, who has existed throughout all eternity. Therefore, if the eternal Son of God came in the likeness of a man, He could not have been born as a result of a physical relationship between a man and woman. Because Jesus is the Son of God, it was absolutely necessary that Jesus be born of a virgin by the power of God's Spirit.

Human life is typically passed on by the male seed. Jesus' birth was the only exception to the normal process of procreation. In fact, when Jesus came into this world it was an entry, not a creation. All other people came through the union of a man to a woman. Jesus was conceived by the Spirit of God.

Teachings Leading to the Understanding That Jesus Is the Son of God:

- We agree that God is Spirit who sees everything and is present everywhere.
- According to the Qur'an, Jesus is the "Spirit from God" (Surah 4:171).
- According to our Christian faith, Jesus is the eternal Spirit, and He took on an additional nature (human nature).
- According to both the Qur'an and the Bible, Jesus was born of a virgin, His mother Mary, without a human father. Jesus is conceived through the Holy Spirit according to both the Qur'an and the Bible. He is not related to any human father.

These teachings help us understand that Jesus could not have been called anything other than the "Son of God." I tell some of my Muslim friends, "If you object that Jesus is the Son of God, then please tell me who His father could be. Please find Him a father." I actually asked this question of two Muslim PhD professors and imams on live Arabic satellite TV viewed by millions of Muslims, and they could not give me an answer.

Now we can see that Jesus' spiritual Sonship to the Father explains the necessity of the virgin birth and gives the reason for it. Please read and consider chapter 27, titled "Jesus Is the Eternal Son of God in a Unique Spiritual Sense," for more details.

Jesus' Virgin Birth Was Prophesied in the Bible

Jesus was born of a virgin as prophesied by the prophet Isaiah seven centuries before Jesus was born (Isaiah 7:14).

The fact that Jesus had this unique beginning to His life on earth proves that He is unique. The virgin birth supports Jesus' divinity. The angel Gabriel (Jibraile) told Mary when he came to explain Jesus' miraculous conception:

"He will be great and will be called the Son of the Most High. . . . The Holy Spirit will come on you, and the power of the Most High will overshadow you. So the holy one to be born will be called the Son of God." (Luke 1:32–35)

15

THE SINLESSNESS OF JESUS CHRIST

N o man or prophet had ever dared to claim himself infallible, but Jesus Christ had complete confidence in His perfection and purity. Therefore, He could boldly ask, "Can any of you prove me guilty of sin? If I am telling the truth, why don't you believe me?" (John 8:46). Jesus' sinlessness was taught throughout the Gospel:

> "He [Jesus] committed no sin, and no deceit was found in his mouth." (1 Peter 2:22)

> "He did not sin." (Hebrews 4:15)

THE QUR'AN SUPPORTS THAT JESUS WAS SINLESS

The only person described as sinless in the Bible, the Qur'an, and the Hadith is Jesus Christ. Jesus was the only man who lived without committing a single sin throughout His life. The Qur'an, in Surah 19:19, states that an angel appeared to Mary and said, "I am only a messenger of thy Lord, that I may bestow on thee a faultless son" (Pickthall). In another translation of the same Surah 19:19, Jesus is described as being "most pure" (Zakeyia).

Al-Baidawi described the Qur'anic phrase, "a boy most pure" as "pure from sins." In Yusuf Ali's translation of this verse, Jesus is referred to as "holy." In Arberry's translation He is referred to as "pure." These are universally accepted translations of the Qur'an.

According to the Hadith (Muhammad), Jesus' sinlessness is very clear. He is the only person who was never influenced by Satan.[1]

MUHAMMAD FELL UNDER THE EFFECT OF EVIL MAGIC

Al-Bukhari noted that even Muhammad fell under the effect of evil spirits.[2] Aisha (one of Muhammad's wives) reported an incident in which Muhammad was imagining he had performed sexual relations with his wives when actually he had not. Then Muhammad prayed to Allah regarding this problem, and Allah answered his prayer by sending two men to him in a dream. Muhammad heard one of them asking the other, "What is wrong with this man [Muhammad]?" The other replied, "He is under the effect of magic."

This Hadith reference goes on to say that Muhammad learned from his dream the identity of the person who performed the evil magic, as well as the material used and its location. Muslim scholars explain that because of the dream God gave to Muhammad, he was able to recognize that he was under the effect of evil magic.

In the Gospel we see that Jesus displayed power over all evil spirits. For example, in Mark 5:1–12, Jesus met a man with an unclean spirit. With divine authority, Jesus commanded the unclean spirit, "Come out of this man, you impure spirit." The man was set free immediately. Therefore, my friend, Jesus is the only One who can protect you and me from the attacks of Satan and his evil spirits.

ALL HAVE SINNED

It is an easy matter to establish from the Bible, the Qur'an, and the Hadith that all people have sinned. Sin resides in every human being. Please consider a few examples:

In the Gospel: According to Romans 3:10, "There is no one righteous, not even one."

In the Hadith: One of the most reliable Hadith says, "Satan circulates in the human mind as blood circulates in it."[3]

It is recorded in the Qur'an, Muhammad said: "Nor do I absolve my own self (of blame): The (human) soul is certainly prone to evil" (Surah 12:5).

References to Sins of the Prophets

In order to show the unique sinlessness of Jesus, it is helpful to consider that the Qur'an and the Bible attribute sin to other great prophets. Here are some references.

Adam

"So by deceit he brought about their fall when they tasted of the tree . . . and their Lord called unto them: 'Did I not forbid you that tree.' . . . They [Adam and Eve] said: 'Our Lord! We have wronged our own souls'" (Surah 7:22–23).

Abraham

Abraham committed the sin of lying because he was afraid (Genesis 12:13).

Abraham asks, "And who, I hope, will forgive me my faults on the Day of Judgment" (Surah 26:82).

Jonah

Jonah disobeyed God (Jonah 1).

"Then the big fish did swallow him [Jonah], and he had done acts worthy of blame" (Surah 37:142).

Moses

Moses disobeyed God (Numbers 20:6–13).

Moses prayed: "O my Lord! I have indeed wronged my soul! Do thou then forgive me!" (Surah 28:16).

Qur'an's References to Muhammad's Sins

It is also significant that the Qur'an attributes sin to Muhammad. Here are several references to Muhammad's sins:

". . . that Allah may forgive thee thy faults of the past and those to follow." (Surah 48:2)

". . . and ask forgiveness for thy fault, and for the men and women who believe . . ." (Surah 47:19)

"and ask forgiveness for thy fault . . ." (Surah 40:55) (See also Surah 4:106 and 110:3.)

It is recorded in the Hadith (Al-Bukhari) that Muhammad said: "By Allah! I ask for forgiveness from Allah and turn to him in repentance more than seventy times a day."[4] In the major works of Hadith there are examples of how Muhammad asked for forgiveness. Al-Bukhari recorded the following prayer by Muhammad: "O, Allah! Wash away my sins with the water of snow and hail, and cleanse my heart from all the sins as a white garment is cleansed from the filth, and let there be a long distance between me and my sins, as You made East and West far from each other."[5] Indeed he continued to ask forgiveness until his last breath.[6]

WHO IS MOST HONORED BY GOD?

It is nowhere stated in the Qur'an, or in the Hadith, or in the Bible that Jesus needed to ask for forgiveness. Even Ayoub Mahmoud M., a noted contemporary Muslim writer, states that Jesus is free from sin. He writes, "Jesus is therefore free from the taint of evil and impurity. . . . This purity, which Adam had until he was touched by Satan's finger and thus lost it, now remains exemplified in Jesus alone."[7]

God would certainly be most pleased with the One who is truly righteous, without sin. Surah 49:13 reads, "Verily the most honored of you in the sight of Allah is (he who is) the most Righteous of you." My dear reader, the most Righteous One is Jesus!

THE REASON FOR THE SINLESSNESS OF JESUS

In the Gospel, Jesus said, "I and the Father are one" (John 10:30). Jesus and God the Father are not the same person, but they are One in essence and nature. Since God the Father and Jesus the Son are One, the Son always does the will of His Father. Jesus said, "Whatever the Father does the Son also does" (John 5:19). Since God the Father would never sin, it follows that Jesus also would not sin.

Because Jesus is one with God, He always did the absolute will of God. He never did anything independently on His own accord. For this reason He never committed a single sin against God or against another human being. Jesus said, "I always do what pleases him" (John 8:29).

Jesus' Nature Was Sinless

Jesus Christ was sinless throughout His earthly life because He was sinless in His nature. Jesus did not have the sin nature that is passed on from Adam to his descendants. Again, He was not conceived by the natural joining of a man and a woman but by the Holy Spirit. We can see now why Jesus is the only Man in human history who lived a sinless life, because He came from God, He is the Son of God!

One week I was speaking in a few churches, and I decided to take some believers with me and go to a mosque to give my book to the Muslims there as a gift. I gave the imam a book, and he looked at it for a few minutes. He said to me, "It is a blasphemy to believe that Jesus is God."

As part of my answer to him, I said, "I am sure that you agree with me, that he who is able to live throughout his life without committing one single sin must be pure and sinless in his nature and essence. Only God is able to exist without sinning, and Jesus also lived his life without committing one single sin. Then He must have the same nature as God. As followers of Jesus, we believe only the facts that God gave us."

Jesus Cleanses Us from All Our Sin

Jesus demonstrated His authority to forgive sins. For example, in Mark 2:1–12, Jesus forgave the paralytic of his sins and healed him. And in Matthew 9:6, Jesus Himself declared that He had the power on earth to forgive sin.

We read in the Gospel:

Jesus said to the paralyzed man, "My child, your sins are forgiven." But some of the teachers of religious law who were sitting there thought to themselves, "What is he saying? This is blasphemy! Only God can forgive sins!" Jesus knew immediately what they were thinking, so he asked them, "Why do you question this in your hearts? Is it easier to say to the paralyzed man 'Your sins are forgiven,' or 'Stand up, pick up your mat, and walk'? So I will prove to you that the Son of Man has the authority on earth to forgive sins." Then Jesus turned to the paralyzed man and said, "Stand up, pick up your mat, and go home!" And the man jumped up, grabbed his mat, and walked out through the stunned onlookers. They were all amazed and praised God, exclaiming, "We've never seen anything like this before!" (Mark 2:5–12 NLT)

My precious reader, please read the beautiful story of the woman caught in the act of adultery (John 8:1–11). The Jewish teachers of the law brought her to Jesus and said she should be stoned to death. Jesus stooped down and wrote in the dust (possibly He wrote their sins), and He told them, "Let the one who has never sinned throw the first stone!" But "they slipped away one by one" (vv. 7, 9 NLT).

Then Jesus stood up again and said to the woman, "Where are your accusers? Didn't even one of them condemn you?"
"No, Lord," she said.
And Jesus said, "Neither do I. Go and sin no more." (John 8:3–11 NLT)

Please notice these significant words by Al-Baidawi regarding Jesus: *"For by his words religion lives, the human soul lives eternally, and people are cleansed from sin."*[8] Jesus is not only sinless, but also cleanses others from their sins. That is why He came to earth. Throughout the Bible we read that the blood of Jesus shed on the cross cleanses us from all sin! (See 1 John 1:7.)

Muslims believe that they should be ritually pure and clean. They wash with clean water before they pray. If they can't find clean water, then they can use sand. And if sand is not available, the person can reach out and touch a clean object to establish the intention that he be purified. My dear friend, clean water can clean only our physical body, but consider the transformation that happens when you reach out in a spiritual sense and believe upon the only pure person—Jesus. At the moment you place your trust in Him and receive Him in your heart as your Savior, His righteousness (purity) will be applied and credited to you, and you will be worthy to stand and kneel before God Almighty!

16

OTHER UNIQUE FEATURES OF JESUS' LIFE

Jesus' ability to raise the dead is taught explicitly in both the Qur'an and the Bible. Raising the dead is a power belonging only to God.

ACCORDING TO THE QUR'AN, JESUS HAS THE POWER TO RAISE THE DEAD

The Qur'an confirms that no one can give life besides God (Surah 15:23; 36:12; and 50:43).

The Qur'an states in explicit language that Jesus actually raised people from the dead. We read in Surah 3:49 that Jesus stated that He raises the dead back to life again.

Surah 5:110 states that God Himself speaks of Jesus' power to raise the dead. According to the Qur'an, this power has been given only to Jesus. And significantly, all Muslim commentators on the Qur'an agree that the power to raise the dead belongs only to God. "He [God] says, 'Who can give life to (dry) bones and decomposed ones (at that)?' Say, 'He [God] will give them life who created them for the first time!'" (Surah 36:78–79).

ACCORDING TO THE BIBLE, JESUS HAS THE POWER TO RAISE THE DEAD

One example is when Lazarus, a close friend of Jesus, died. Jesus declared to Lazarus's sister Martha, "I am the resurrection and the life. Anyone who believes in me will live, even after dying" (John 11:25 NLT). Then Jesus raised Lazarus from the dead.

Jesus came to conquer death and give eternal life to whoever believes in Him.

JESUS HAS POWER OVER DEATH

In the Gospel, Jesus Himself declares that He has power over death. His words are recorded in the Gospel according to John:

"For just as the Father raises the dead and gives them life, even so the Son gives life to whom he is pleased to give it" (John 5:21).

"And this is the will of him who sent me, that I shall lose none of all those he has given me, but raise them up at the last day" (John 6:39; see also verse 44).

Jesus proved that He possesses absolute power over life and death!

ACCORDING TO THE QUR'AN, JESUS HAS THE ABILITY TO CREATE LIFE

The Qur'an clearly states that God is the one who creates all things. The Qur'an confirms that only the true and living God has the ability to create. This belief is noted in Surah 15:86; 16:17, 20; and 22:73. It is curious to read in Surah 3:49 that Jesus created living beings (birds) out of clay by breathing into them (Jesus' breath gave life to the clay). This is the same way that God created Adam! (See also Surah 5:110.) Also the same verse confirms that Jesus gave the ability to see, for those who were born blind.

While these are interesting statements about what the Qur'an says about Jesus as life-giver, Christians would only take the Bible as authoritative on what miracles can be ascribed to Jesus.

JESUS HAS THE ABILITY TO KNOW THE UNSEEN

Jesus has the ability to know the unseen, according to the Qur'an and the Bible. The knowledge of the unseen (that which cannot be seen by human eyes) is a divine quality. As the Qur'an states, "With Him are the keys of the unseen, the treasures that none knoweth but He" (Surah 6:59). The Qur'an also states: "Say: none in the heavens or on earth, except Allah, knows what is hidden" (Surah 27:65).

Muhammad himself stated in the Qur'an that he did not possess the knowledge of the unseen: "If I had knowledge of the unseen, I should have multiplied all good, and no evil should have touched me" (Surah 7:188). (See also Surah 6:50 and Surah 11:31.)

According to the Qur'an in Surah 3:49, God granted the ability to know the unseen only to Jesus. Jesus had the ability to know even the small details of people's lives. According to the Gospel, Jesus even knows the thoughts and the intents of man's heart. John 2:24–25 states, "But Jesus would not entrust himself to them, for he knew all people. . . . For he knew what was in each person."

We also learn from the Gospel that Jesus, as a prophet, knew unseen future events, such as His death and resurrection (Matthew 16:21).

Jesus Has Power to Provide Food

The Qur'an states in Surah 51:58 that God is the only One who can give sustenance. A prominent early Muslim scholar, Ibn Kathir, explained that Christ had the ability to give sustenance to whomever He wished.

Clearly we see Christ's ability to provide food when He fed the five thousand people with a few loaves of bread and a couple of fish (Luke 9:12–17).

MORE UNIQUE FEATURES OF JESUS' LIFE AS RECORDED IN THE QUR'AN

Jesus Was Continuously Accompanied by the Holy Spirit

Surah 2:87 says, "We gave Jesus, the Son of Mary, clear (Signs) and strengthened him with the Holy Spirit." According to the Qur'an and the writings of Muslim scholars, Jesus was the only person who was continuously accompanied by the Holy Spirit from His conception to His ascension. We see that Jesus has the capacity to enjoy ongoing and total harmony and companionship with the Holy Spirit.

Jesus Is Forever Eminent

Jesus is the only person described as being eminent in this world and in the next. In the Qur'an (in Surah 3:45), we read, "Behold! The angels said: 'O Mary! Allah giveth thee Glad tidings of a Word from Him: his name will be Christ Jesus. The Son of Mary, held in honor [*wajih*] in this world and the hereafter and of (the company of) those nearest to Allah.'"

The Arabic word *wajih* in the above verse is also translated "eminent" in other translations of the Qur'an. In commenting on this Surah 3:45, the well known Muslim scholar Shukani explains that "eminence is power and authority."[1]

Al-Razi, another prominent Muslim scholar, comments on Surah 3:45: "Jesus is distinguished (wajih) in this life, because his requests are granted, he raised the dead, healed the blind. . . . He is distinguished in the life to come because He (God) made him intercede on behalf of his true people, and (God) accepts his intercession for them."[2]

Jesus Is the Intercessor

The Gospel assures that Jesus is continually interceding for His followers (believers) before God the Father. "Because Jesus lives forever . . . he is able to save completely those who come to God through him, because he always lives to intercede for them" (Hebrews 7:24–25).

My Muslim friend, I know that you want to please God, because you have already read so many pages of my book. I encourage you to put your faith in Jesus right now and decide to follow Him and His teachings. I urge you to go to Jesus and ask Him to intercede for you.

WHY WAS IT NECESSARY FOR JESUS TO COME?

17

THE PROBLEM OF SIN

In this chapter, my friend, we will observe the problem of our sinful condition and God's solution to it.

MAN'S SINFUL CONDITION

First, let us look at some of the passages in the Qur'an that confirm the sinfulness of all human beings:

- "The (human) soul is certainly prone to evil" (Surah 12:53).
- "Verily, man is given up to injustice and ingratitude" (Surah 14:34).
- "Truly man is, to his Lord, ungrateful" (Surah 100:6).
- Most men will not believe in God. "Most men believe not" (Surah 13:1). (See also Surah 12:103, 106; Surah 15:10–11.)
- "Man doth transgress all bounds" (Surah 96:6).
- "He has created man. . . . And behold this same (man) becomes an open disputer!" (Surah 16:4).

The Bible certainly confirms the fact that all of us have sinned. It declares, "For all [people] have sinned" (Romans 3:23).

Prophet David (Daud) said, "Surely I was sinful at birth, sinful from the time my mother conceived me" (Psalm 51:5). David also prayed, "Do not bring your servant into judgment, for no one living is righteous before you" (Psalm 143:2).

The Hadith confirms this truth—the sinfulness of all human beings. It is recorded in one of the most acknowledged Hadith that Muhammad, the prophet of Islam, said, "Satan circulates in the human mind as blood circulates in it."[1] Muhammad also said, "Adam's every son is sinful."[2]

Imam Khamenei, at his inauguration as president of Iran on September 4, 1985, made some comments on man and said, "If the whole world is gathered and given to him, he will not feel satisfied. You see that the mighty who have great power seek more power. . . . Arrogance should be stopped and ego should be controlled in everything. The downfall of man is that he wants absolute power" (i.e., the power of God).[3]

Khomeini confirmed his point by further saying, "You should pay attention and all of us should pay attention [to the fact] that man's calamity is his carnal desires, and this exists in everybody, and it is rooted in the nature of man."[4]

If people are essentially pure—as most Muslim scholars teach —how can we ignore all the evidence that proves the opposite?

Those who teach that man is a fundamentally good and pure creature are not teaching the truth.

I encourage you, my dear Muslim reader, to examine the evidence.

What Is Sin?

Sin is disobeying God by committing acts against His will, and it begins with evil thoughts. Jesus said, "For out of the heart come evil thoughts—murder, adultery, sexual immorality, theft, false testimony, slander. These are what defile a person" (Matthew 15:19–20). Jesus taught us that it is far more important to be clean on the inside than on the outside (Matthew 23:25–28). The Bible explains that the root of all sin is selfishness. Sin is a condition of our human nature that is not in harmony with the will of God. We don't always do what God wants us to do, and we do things that God does not want us to do. When we hurt ourselves we sin because God owns our life.

The unfortunate reality is that human nature's tendency to sin is a compelling force. Obviously it is naive to think that people are basically good and pure. If sin is merely a choice that a person makes, then why is no one able to keep a promise to God to do all according to His will and submit to Him always through perfect obedience? I am sure you would agree that no one is able to live up to a perfect commitment and never sin again.

An Illustration of Sin

Our sinful nature manifests itself through our thoughts, actions, and words. Our entire being (including the mind, heart, mouth, eyes, etc.) is infected by the sin virus that makes us impure before God.

My dear Muslim friend, imagine, for example, that you are at the market. You are given a choice of three meat mixtures. The first has 50 percent beef and 50 percent pork. The next has 90 percent beef and 10 percent pork. The third has 99 percent beef and 1 percent pork. Which one would you buy? As a devout Muslim, you would refuse them all because Islam teaches that any amount of pork, no matter how insignificant, makes the meat *haram* (unlawful to eat). That is how sin is; no matter how small we think our sins are, they put us in a state of defiance to God and His will. Thus we become *unacceptable* in God's eyes!

Sin makes us unable to obtain God's approval and unworthy to enter paradise.

No person can depend on self to become clean before God. It is really arrogant to think one can be good enough for God.

Sin Makes Us Unclean

According to the Islamic teaching and beliefs, if someone were to wash all his body in preparation to pray, and before he started his prayer some dust fell on him, ritually he would be considered unclean. God would not accept his prayers. As a Muslim, if you believe that some dust on your physical body will disqualify you from praying, then you should be able to accept the biblical truth that the dirt of sin within us makes us unclean. Even a tiny speck of sin disqualifies us from approaching the holy God. Remember, Adam and Eve lost the ability to be in the presence of God because of one single sin.

The pure, just, and holy God cannot accept us into heaven on the basis of our good works. Our lives contain various selfish and sinful deeds that good works cannot erase. God will not allow any defiled or impure person to enter Paradise. God considers "partial obedience" as disobedience.

Human efforts to be clean always fall short. God cannot accept us in our unclean or sinful state.

According to the Qur'an, Everyone Is Going to Hell

The Qur'an mentions hell fire in Surah 19:71, "Not one of you but will pass over it [hell fire]: this is, with Thy Lord, a Decree which must be accomplished." In a different Qur'anic translation of the same verse, the expression "pass through it" is used. This is a translation of the Arabic word *wardha*; however, this word literally means "enter it." Many Muslims ask whether this verse refers just to the wicked or includes all men. The Suyuti tells us that Muhammad himself answered this question by saying, "There is no righteous or debaucher who would not enter hell."[5]

The Qur'an Offers No Eternal Security

Tragically, according to the Qur'an and the Hadith, no Muslim can be sure of what to expect after death. According to Al-Bukhari, Muhammad, the prophet of Islam, said, "By Allah, though I am The Apostle of Allah, yet I do not know what Allah will do to me."[6]

God as described in the Qur'an does not guarantee the Muslim believer forgiveness of sins, acceptance, or eternal life with him.

WHAT SHOULD A RIGHTEOUS JUDGE DO?

Our sins violate the will and law of God. They are an insult to God and harmful to those He created and loves. Since God is holy and just, the sinner deserves His judgment. God would not be fair and just unless He was to punish the sinner. Repentance alone, which is a return to the place of obedience, cannot remove past sins, nor can it satisfy the holiness and justice of God, even if we were to add our good works to it.

Imagine that a young man attacked a woman physically and was standing before a judge. The man pleads, "I repent and I am very sorry for what I did and I will never do it again. Your Honor, I promise to be nice and respectful toward all the women I meet for the rest of my life. I will donate much of my time and money to help victims of rape. As a matter of fact, Your Honor, I can prove I did many, many good deeds before and after this crime. Your Honor, I am really sorry for the wrong I did, and I am sorry I broke the law. Since I have done many good deeds and I plan to do more, I am asking you to grant me a pardon. Forgive me and set me free."

How do you think the judge should respond? The judge should say, "Although I appreciate your good deeds and apology, I must deal with your crime by issuing a punishment."

God Will Judge Each Person for His or Her Sins

My beloved Muslim reader, it will be the same when we stand before God on the day of judgment. Because of His holiness and justice, He has to deal with our sins. Eternal punishment is certain for those whose sins are not forgiven.

Again, repentance and good works do not eradicate the effect of sin or guilt. While obedience requires good works, we cannot use our good works to erase our bad deeds. In other words, good works are a requirement of obedience but not a solution to sin!

It is recorded in Al-Bukhari that Muhammad said to a group of people, "The deeds of any one of you will not save you (from the hell fire)." Then they asked him, "Even you (will not be saved by your deeds), O Allah's Apostle?" He responded, "No, even I (will not be saved) unless and until Allah bestows His mercy on me."[7] Muhammad also said, "The good deeds of any person will not make him enter Paradise."[8]

The Qur'an states, "Allah called them to account for their sins. For Allah is strict in punishment" (Surah 3:11).

Sin Requires Payment

Dishonoring the mayor is a big mistake. Dishonoring the president is certainly a bigger mistake. Dishonoring the perfect God is an infinite mistake that places us in a state of infinite debt. We cannot pay such a debt.

If I wronged a colleague with whom I worked, another colleague could help me to reconcile with the one I wronged.

If I wronged the president and owner of the company for whom I worked, my colleague could not intercede between the president and me. He could not help me. I would need someone very influential, someone to whom the president would consider it important to listen.

When you or I sin against God, we need Jesus to intercede for us.

GOD MADE IT POSSIBLE FOR US TO BECOME RIGHTEOUS THROUGH FAITH

The Bible tells us,
The whole world [is] held accountable to God.

Therefore no one will be declared righteous in God's sight by the works of the law; rather, through the law we become conscious of our sin. But now apart from the law the righteousness of God has been made known, to which the Law and the Prophets testify. This righteousness is given through faith in Jesus Christ to all who believe. There is no difference between Jew and Gentile, for all have sinned and fall short of the glory of God, and all are justified freely by his grace through the redemption that came by Christ Jesus. (Romans 3:19–24)

God's law is a reflection of His perfect standard. God's law declares us guilty. The law shows us how far from perfect we really are.

We will not be able to plead innocence because we are not innocent of sin. In the just courtroom of heaven, before God the righteous and just Judge, we stand. The verdict? Guilty. We deserve eternal punishment.

My Wife's Story

The law reveals our sin like the mirror shows us exactly how we look. The law shows us God's standard and our inability to live up to it. But the law cannot make us righteous.

True submission to God is to humble ourselves before Him, realizing His holiness, and confessing our sins and shortcomings. Honoring God is knowing our unworthiness and accepting His provision.

God is offering you salvation through faith. God is the One who saves you. Placing your trust in Jesus is the means by which you accept God's grace. If you reject God's gracious offer now, you will one day have to face His righteous judgment according to His law.

I would like to share with you that my wife was born and raised in Egypt as a devout Muslim. She graduated from a prestigious Islamic university (Azhar), majoring in Islamic study and Arabic language. She was a teacher of Arabic and Islamic religion. She was always trying to gain God's favor through her works. Her life changed when she put her faith in what God has done for her through Jesus Christ.

My wife's faith is genuine. She suffered and was thrown in prison because she refused to deny Jesus Christ. She almost lost her life, but Jesus was protecting and comforting her during her time in prison. She met three other ex-Muslims in prison. They joined my wife in prayers and singing praise songs to God every day. God used all of them to help some prisoners experience God's love and salvation.

God's Forgiveness Is a Gift

God inspired David to write, "Blessed is the one whose transgressions are forgiven, whose sins are covered. Blessed is the one whose sin the LORD does not count against them" (Psalm 32:1–2).

A verse in the Qur'an shows our need for God to make us righteous and that we do not have the solution to our sin problem: "Our Lord! We have heard the call of one calling (us) to faith, 'Believe ye in the Lord,' and we have believed. Our Lord! Forgive us our sins, blot out from us our iniquities, and take to thyself our souls in the company of the righteous" (Surah 3:193).

God gave you free will and freedom of choice. You have made wrong choices and disobeyed Him. You sinned willfully. The cost of the damages you did is more than you can pay. Divine rescue is necessary. God, the heavenly Father, paid the price Himself. The moment you trust Christ as your Savior, you are granted immunity from punishment and the case against you is closed.

All the penalty and death we deserve for our sins fell upon Jesus. Through God's divine self-sacrifice, God manifested His divine love for you and me, which triumphed over His divine wrath toward us (sinners).

God will justify you only when you accept His own payment for all of your sins. I clearly remember struggling as if I were climbing a mountain with a heavy backpack. On February 17, 1976, I repented and put my faith in Jesus Christ as my Savior. I felt so light, so free, so forgiven.

Jesus Paid the Penalty for Our Sins

Jesus Christ removed the barrier between man and God. The Bible notes, "This is love: not that we loved God, but that he loved us and sent his Son as an *atoning sacrifice* for our sins" (1 John 4:10, italics added). Out of matchless love for us, God placed our sin debt on Jesus, who willingly took our place as the sacrifice for us.

Remember, my friend, that none of us can say with a clear

conscience, "I am not a sinner." It only takes one sin to become a sinner. In addition, as previously expounded, our fallen sinful nature guarantees that everyone will sin again to some degree. Trying to deal with difficult situations, trying to enjoy moments of pleasure, and simply living with a sinful nature leads you to commit sin.

Are you willing, like me, to admit that you have sinned and you are a sinner who cannot earn your way to heaven? Will you acknowledge that you are in need of God's mercy and grace?

Illustration of God's Gift of Grace

God wants you to obtain and enjoy His salvation—as a gift. If you tried to earn it by your efforts, you could not because you do not deserve it. But if you ask God to save you, He will do so gladly because He loves you.

The following story demonstrates God's gift of grace:

There once was a poor and hungry woman. While she was tired from walking, she saw a garden full of fruits. She tried to pay the gardener some money to sell her some fruit. But he refused the money.

Each time she attempted to buy the fruit, her offer was refused. But the woman continued to plead with the gardener to take her money. Then one day the prince, the king's son, overheard the woman begging. After he learned the situation, the kind prince told the woman, "My father the king owns this garden. He is not a merchant and does not need your money. You cannot buy his fruit, but he will give it freely to you if you merely ask and believe in his free gift." The woman joyfully accepted the king's gracious offer. Then the prince picked an abundance of the most perfect fruit and gave the woman all she needed!

God knows we are unable to save ourselves. Because of His deep and amazing love toward us, He offers us salvation as a gift. "For it is by *grace* you have been saved, through faith—and this not from yourselves, it is the gift of God—not by works, so that no one can boast" (Ephesians 2:8–9, italics added).

Realizing that we are desperately in need of God's grace humbles us, and receiving God's grace uplifts us.

I remember when I was a child I would occasionally get into trouble. My father owned the building where we lived in Egypt. His legal practice was on the ground floor while we resided upstairs. Many times I invited my friends over to play soccer in the hallway on the ground floor. On one occasion, our ball broke a lightbulb. And another time, it hit one of my father's clients. Sometimes the ball would even hit the glass door of my father's office. These disturbances, along with the joyful yelling and screaming, often interrupted his business conversations.

When my father finished work and entered our home with that certain look that told me I was in trouble, I would run to my mother crying. I would hide behind her, trusting that because of her I would be safe and forgiven. Although he was angry, many times he would see my mother's beautiful face and my repentant heart and let me go unpunished. Other times, my mother would gather me in her arms and shield me with her big body.

This memory always reminds me of when I ran to Jesus in February 1976 and put my trust in Him; I experienced God's forgiveness. Jesus covered me with His righteousness, shielding me from punishment.

The Bible states, "It is by the name of Jesus Christ. . . . Salvation is found in no one else, for there is no other name under heaven given to mankind by which we must be saved" (Acts 4:10, 12).

My dear reader, you need to drink from God's grace so your soul can be satisfied. Then you will have an unimaginable inner peace filling your innermost being. God knocks softly on the door of your heart. If you were to ask me, "Samy, how do you know?" I would answer, "He knocked on the door of my heart years ago and I invited Him in. I have not been the same since because He continues to fill me with peace and love." Can you hear Him knocking? He desires to have fellowship with you. Will you open the door for Him by faith and allow Him to enter your life and be your Lord and friend? God is inviting you to cast yourself on His grace, mercy, love, and forgiveness.

Salvation Is Immediate!

Even if you are one of the worst sinners, you can be forgiven and saved today! While Jesus hung on the cross, He told a sinful criminal hanging on the cross next to Him, "Today you will be with me in paradise" (Luke 23:43). God knew this sinner (who expressed his faith in Jesus) would die with no time left to complete any good works. God knew his believing and repentant heart.

True Christians Do Not Want to Continue in Sin

There are many people today who claim to be Christians. They call themselves Christians but live a sinful lifestyle. These people are deceived, for the true believers and followers of Jesus Christ obey His teaching and submit continually to God.

The forgiveness of sin does not give Christians the right to continue in sin. No true follower of Christ purposely continues to live in sin.

Christ gives His true followers the desire and power to do good. Titus 2:14 notes that Jesus "gave himself for us to redeem us from all wickedness and to purify for himself a people that are his very own, eager to do what is good."

Some Muslims incorrectly teach that Christians do not care about doing good works because of their dependence on what

Jesus has done for them. The Gospel teaches believers to "pray continually" (1 Thessalonians 5:17). Thus, all true Christians who follow the teachings of the Bible know they are to remain in fellowship with God, surrendering their lives to Him and submitting to His will continually.

It is also true that since the coming of Jesus until today, in every generation, multitudes of Christians lived and sacrificed their lives to serve God and serve people.

Regarding prayer Jesus Himself taught,

> "When you pray, do not be like the hypocrites, for they love to pray standing in the synagogues and on the street corners to be seen by others. Truly I tell you, they have received their reward in full. But when you pray, go into your room, close the door and pray to your Father, who is unseen. Then your Father, who sees what is done in secret, will reward you." (Matthew 6:5–6)

Jesus taught a similar message about fasting (in verses 16–17).

Spiritual Growth for the Christian Is a Process

Just as infants grow physically, people who are "born again" (through faith in Jesus) grow spiritually. Followers of Christ stumble and fall short of the perfect standard of their holy God. They struggle against sin, the desires of the flesh, and Satan. Gradually they mature in their spiritual lives. When Christians grieve about their sins, they can take comfort in God's promise to always forgive them when they confess and repent. This glorious promise is found in 1 John 1:9: "If we confess our sins, he is faithful and just and will forgive us our sins and purify us from all unrighteousness."

Believers in Christ rejoice that God does not leave them to struggle alone. The Holy Spirit empowers them to overcome temptations and changes their character to be more like Jesus. Thus they become more loving, forgiving, and willing to obey and serve God. "For it is God who works in you to will and to act in order to fulfill his good purpose" (Philippians 2:13).

The Bible assures us that God, who starts a good work in each believer, is faithful to complete it (Philippians 1:6). The Holy Spirit within the believer produces good works and wonderful traits. We read in the Bible, "The fruit of the Spirit is love, joy, peace, forbearance, kindness, goodness, faithfulness, gentleness and self-control" (Galatians 5:22–23a).

The Bible tells us that God is constantly working in us, to change us to be the people He created us to be.

Farid Esack, a renowned Muslim scholar and one who enjoyed the position of the Brueggeman Chair in Interreligious Studies at Xavier University in Cincinnati, Ohio, wrote, "One can be totally committed to Islam and yet not have it touch one's inner being.... Our lives as Muslims are largely devoid of an ongoing and living connection with Allah."[9]

18

GOD HIMSELF CAME TO US IN THE PERSON OF JESUS, THE MESSIAH

The Gospel teaches that God chose to enter our world in the person of Jesus, who was conceived by the Holy Spirit in the body of a virgin. Jesus remained pure and sinless as He expressed God's wonderful love for the human race.

GOD IS BOTH MIGHTY AND HUMBLE

Some people say, "Jesus ate, drank, and slept while He lived on earth. How can Jesus be God, since God does not need to do any of these activities that humans do?"

It is true that God does not have to do any of these human activities, just like a king does not have to sleep where his servants sleep or eat with them. He certainly does not have to go through such humbling experiences. However, he can choose to do so if he wants to get close to his servants to experience their feelings and ultimately solve their problems. He can choose to spend time with them in their environment.

Likewise, the God of the Bible is the Servant-King. Would we dare to place boundaries upon God's power and will? Are we not limiting God by saying He is unable to express Himself in human form? Man certainly could not become Almighty God. But God certainly could come to our world and manifest Himself through the perfect man, Jesus Christ.

Spirit Beings Can Take on Human Form

Take note: the Qur'an states that the Spirit of God can appear in human form. An example is in Surah 19:17, "We sent to her Our Spirit (Ruhana), and he appeared before her as a man in all respects."

The Bible and the Qur'an both acknowledge that God at times sends His angels, who are spirit in form (*ruh*), in the exact likeness of human appearance. So there is no reasonable argument from the Qur'an against the *possibility* that Jesus, who likewise is Spirit in form, took on actual human form.

God Desires to Associate Closely with People

Many Muslim scholars, such as Assfy, point out that "God does not have to be associated in any way with men."[1] Of course this statement is true. God, however, reveals Himself in the Gospel to be a God of love who desires to meet us at our level and graciously identify with us closely. He is a God who longs for us to come to Him so He can embrace us and communicate with us through His Spirit, which He will send to dwell within us. He wants to adopt us as children and become our loving, heavenly Father.

158

GOD IS ALMIGHTY AND PRESENT EVERYWHERE

The Qur'an states in Surah 55:14: "He [Allah] created man from . . . clay like unto pottery." This verse indicates that God made Adam at a specific time by holding in His hand clay from a specific place on the earth.

The Qur'an also states that God personally talked to Adam and taught Adam the names of all things (Surah 2:31). And in the Bible, we learn that God walked in the garden of Eden and communicated with Adam and Eve (Genesis 3:8). These events did not confine Him, because God is almighty and present everywhere. In the same way, God's incarnation (coming in the form of a man) at a specific time and place did not confine Him. He remains the almighty, sovereign God who fills the whole universe with His presence and yet desires to fellowship with us one-on-one.

Our Loving God Desires to Communicate to Us Personally

Muslims agree with Christians that, ultimately, God can only be known through His self-revelations. The Bible declares that God came to us through the person of Jesus Christ, taking on human nature to reveal the infinite in a language the finite can understand.

Please consider this hypothetical situation: If you desired to communicate with a bird and you had unlimited power and authority, what would be the best way for you to do so? The answer is that you would become a bird! Then you could communicate on the same level.

Please consider another illustration: During the Vietnam War, a certain family was separated. While the wife and two boys were able to move to the United States, the father was forced to stay in Vietnam. For many years they communicated with each other only through letters and pictures. The father could watch his boys grow up only from a distance. Then, finally, the governments of Vietnam and the United States allowed the father to come to the United States to be with his family.

What if the father had said to his family, "I don't really see any need to visit you in person? Communicating through letters and pictures will continue to be sufficient for me." What would you think of such a father? Likewise, what would you think of a God who was able to communicate with and visit His creation in person, but refused to do so?

God's Divine Nature Is Never Lessened

My dear Muslim reader, Almighty God is able to appear in the person of the Messiah and to personally speak to mankind without lessening His essence or staining His divine character. According to the Gospel, Jesus' life on earth was a perfect demonstration of God's love, forgiveness, holiness, healing, power, and salvation.

Also remember that all the bodily functions of a human being are God's design and are pure as long as they are used according to His will.

Jesus Christ, the Word of God, did not lose His divine nature when He became a human. According to both the Qur'an and the Gospel, He raised the dead, healed the lepers, and gave sight to the blind. He had many other divine characteristics that cannot be attributed to a mere human being. Many of these are introduced in later chapters.

Could the Creator of all things including the human body visit our world and present Himself to save us without being impaired in any way? Of course He could! On one occasion, Jesus told His disciples, "With man, this is impossible, but with God all things are possible" (Matthew 19:26).

Please, allow me to give you an illustration.

Before one Labor Day holiday, the president of the United States spent several hours wearing a factory uniform as he talked with and labored alongside hardworking steel manufacturers. He really did put in an honest day's work. By the end of the shift, his clothes were dirty and smelly.

The president was not less honorable because of what he did. On the contrary, his humble spirit and actions honored him, the factory workers, every worker in America, and also America itself.

The Humanity of Jesus

The Gospel contains many statements showing us that Jesus' body on earth was a real human body. His humanity was obvious in that Jesus was hungry, tempted, and crucified. He walked and talked with His disciples and others. He suffered mental anguish and physical pain. He was fully human.

The Deity of Jesus

The Gospel includes many statements indicating the deity of Jesus. For example, Jesus is

- Eternal (everlasting): He existed before the world was formed (John 8:58; 17:5).
- Ever-Present: He is present everywhere at all times (Matthew 18:20).
- All-Knowing: He demonstrated knowledge of things that could only be known if He were divine (Matthew 9:4; Matthew 11:27; Luke 6:8; John 4:29).
- All-Powerful: He demonstrated unlimited, supernatural power and authority (Matthew 8:23–27; 28:18; Mark 5:11–15).

Jesus, Fully Human and Fully Divine

Some Muslims ask, "How is it possible for the divine nature to be united with the human nature in the life of Jesus?" I answer, "Whatever the Almighty God decides to do according to His infinite wisdom, He is able to accomplish."

It might be helpful to think of the union between the soul and the body. In this analogy, the nature of the soul unites with the physical earthly nature of the body to form a union of one nature, which is the human nature.

This united nature does not include the body alone nor the soul alone, but both together are combined without mixing, alteration, or transmutation (change). The soul and the body become one in essence and in nature, one person.

This dual nature of Jesus is unimaginable to our limited human mind, but there are many other things we don't fully understand. How is it possible for spirit and flesh to be united in us? The creation of the first human was also a mystery. God made man (His vice regent on earth) by using mud and His divine breath. Therefore, we should not consider it a strange thing that the second man, whom God sent to be our Savior, the Messiah Jesus, had both divine and human nature.

In many cases two truths, which seemed completely contradictory to us at one time, are now, after we have gained more knowledge and spiritual light (insight), understood to be in harmony. Also we need to acknowledge that truths that still seem to us to be contradictory may perfectly harmonize according to God's infinite wisdom, and we will someday understand them.

The union of the divine with human form took place in Christ for the purpose of satisfying God's justice, manifesting His love for us, and accomplishing our salvation.

The divine nature of God did not change and become human

nature, and the human nature of Jesus did not change and become divine nature. This union is not a blend, but rather the human nature and the divine nature existed together in the person and life of Jesus Christ without change or blending together.

The divine nature remained divine and the human nature remained human.

Man Was Created in God's Image

My dear Muslim friend, God chose to save us. He accomplished this goal by appearing in the form of a perfect, sinless man to be our personal Savior. God did not become incarnate in a plant, a bird, or an animal because they do not bear His image. But we know from the Torah that God created us in His image. "God said, 'Let us make mankind in our image'" (Genesis 1:26). The Qur'an in Surah 15:29 states, "When I have fashioned him and breathed into him [only into man] of My Spirit . . ."

Biblical scholar Bedru Kateregga explains that "man created in the image of God does not mean that God looks like man or that man looks like God. But it does mean that man has profound God-like qualities."[2] For example, God created man with the ability to be loving, just, and compassionate. It is interesting that all of us are aware that we should act better and that we can become better humans. Kateregga continues, "This is the witness of our God—likeness within our conscience. It is a persistent voice in the conscience that we should become better people, that we do not always do what we know we should do, that we really should be more kind, true, reliable, pure, more God-like."[3] It is also Godlike to be humble and to love sacrificially.

In harmony with what I just mentioned, Muhammad said, "Allah created Adam in His picture."[4]

JESUS IS THE PERFECT MEDIATOR

Jesus, the Messiah, is the perfect Mediator between God and man. The Bible declares, "This is good, and pleases God our Savior, who wants all people to be saved and to come to a knowledge of the truth. For there is one God and one mediator between God and mankind, the man Christ Jesus, who gave himself as a ransom for all people" (1 Timothy 2:3–6). Only Christ could be called the perfect and acceptable sacrifice to God. In Him we see all the necessary characteristics that must be found in the Mediator (Savior).

The Savior Must Be Human

How could God—who is Spirit—pay the penalty for the sins of man who is flesh? It was a human penalty He wanted to bear. Therefore, God acquired human form, became a true member of the human race, and paid the penalty. As a man, Christ could represent humanity.

Jesus understands our struggles because He faced them as a human being on earth.

The Savior Must Be Divine

Who can pay the full price (penalty) for all the sins people have committed? Therefore, the sacrifice had to have an infinite value. Everything Jesus did derived unique significance from His divine identity. The Savior descended to us from God so He could lift us up to God.

The Savior Unites You with God

The Bible states, "For in Christ lives all the fullness of God in a human body" (Colossians 2:9 NLT). Jesus promised, "Here I am!

I stand at the door [of your heart] and knock. If anyone hears my voice and opens the door, I will come in" (Revelation 3:20).

My precious reader, this means that God Himself will live within you when you invite Jesus to enter your heart and life. Since Jesus shares the very nature of God and He offers to live within you, He is able to unite you with God.

Therefore, the moment you believe in who Jesus is and invite Him to enter your life, He will enter your life and through His Spirit He will give you the abundant, rich life God created you to enjoy. You will be full of life. You will be more alive than ever. God guarantees this. Jesus said: "I am . . . the life" (John 14:6).

Jesus alone qualified as the connecting link between God and man. The gulf between heaven and earth was bridged by the coming of Jesus. None but Jesus Christ could give spiritual and eternal life to all those who believe in Him.

The union of divinity and humanity—in the person of Jesus—made it possible for man and God to be united forever!

Jesus prayed, "I pray also for those who will believe in me . . . Father, just as you are in me and I am in you. May they also be in us . . . I in them and you in me" (John 17:20–23). A marvelous transformation and inheritance awaits you when you believe in Jesus.

My precious reader, God wants to be united to you, to give you Himself, and share with you all He has. I would like to share a true story of a wealthy couple. They sat down with a marriage counselor in his office to solve their marital problems. Angrily, the husband said, "I don't understand my wife's problem. I gave her a diamond ring for our wedding anniversary, I bought a house in her name, and I gave her money to spend on herself every month." After he listed everything he gave her, the wife replied, "Yes it is true, Ameer, you have given me everything."

With tears running from her eyes, she continued, "Everything except yourself!"

It is my hope and prayer that through reading this book you will see how God has actually given you the ultimate gift of love—Himself! "This is how we know what love is: Jesus Christ laid down his life for us" (1 John 3:16).

19

THE INCARNATION
OF JESUS

The Bible explains in Philippians 2:5–9:

> Have the same mindset as Christ Jesus: Who, being in very
> nature God . . . made himself nothing by taking the very
> nature of a servant, being made in human likeness. And
> being found in appearance as a man, he humbled himself by
> becoming obedient to death—even death on a cross! There-
> fore God exalted him to the highest place and gave him the
> name that is above every name.

This passage in Philippians reveal truths about the nature
and work of Christ. "Being in very nature God" refers to Christ's
divine nature. I have mentioned before that Christ is united to
God in one Spirit throughout eternity. When Christ came to
earth through the Virgin Mary, He humbly took on an additional
nature (a human nature) and appeared in our world as a man. He

has two natures—one divine and one human—that were unified in one person.

JESUS SUBMITTED TO THE FATHER'S WILL

The passage continues by saying Jesus "made Himself nothing," which does not mean He gave up or surrendered His divine nature. It means He voluntarily submitted Himself to serve the will of the Father. And He took "the very nature of a servant."

This passage in Philippians reminds me of a story I read of a noble king whose kingdom was invaded by an evil enemy. The enemy captured many of his people and used them as slaves in a remote land. The king's only son, the prince, agreed with his father's desire that he be sent to this remote place. The prince wore the clothes of a common person, went where his people suffered as slaves, and lived with them. Then at the right time the prince used his power and influence and set his people free from the captivity of the enemy. The son labored and sacrificed for the benefit of his father's kingdom. The son restored the honor of his father and his kingdom.

We read in the Bible about Jesus: "For you know the grace of our Lord Jesus Christ, that though he was rich, yet for your sake he became poor, so that you through his poverty might become rich" (2 Corinthians 8:9).

Note that while He lived on earth, Christ's glory remained veiled to most people. He used His divine power only according to the will of the Father. He did not use His supernatural powers to alleviate His own human suffering or for any personal gain (Matthew 8:20).

THE PURPOSE OF JESUS' COMING (INCARNATION)

- God revealed Himself to us in Jesus, so we can know Him. Jesus said to His Father: "I have made you known to them, and will continue to make you known" (John 17:26). It takes God to reveal God.
- Jesus provided an example for our lives by His living in total submission to God's will. We are told in the Bible to "live as Jesus did" (1 John 2:6).
- Jesus taught us, "Do to others as you would like them to do to you" (Luke 6:31 NLT).
- Jesus taught us to serve one another. For example, when He washed and dried the feet of His disciples, He said to them, "I have set you an example that you should do as I have done for you" (John 13:15).

The incarnation of Jesus opens our eyes to the value God places on human life. It assures us of the powerful, deep love God has for you and me. He even came for us while we were still in our sinful and fallen state.

God is just. The Judge of all the earth had to do right. Sin was a violation of the holy Law of God according to God's moral order. Therefore, it was impossible for God to deal lightly with sin. Forgiveness of sin had to be on the basis that would satisfy the perfect standard of the holiness and justice of God. Jesus assumed our human position, and in the form of man took the entire burden (judgment) of our sin upon Himself. Through the sacrifice of Jesus Christ, God satisfied His righteous justice. We see in Christ both the judgment and the mercy of God. We see God as both the *Just* and the *Justifier*.

God made it possible for our sins to be pardoned without

endorsing them. God cannot condone our sins, for He cannot lower His holy standard.

Since all men are sinners, God Himself had to provide the sinless man. Jesus paid the price for us when He willingly bore the punishment in our place. God is still God and the consequence of sin is still death. Through Jesus, however, we can be saved and have eternal life. Glory to God!

Before you read more glad news, please stop and say a prayer. Ask God to guide you to His truth, to an understanding of His Word. Believe that God desires to pour out His love on you. You might be thinking you don't deserve God's love. None of us deserves God's awesome love. The Bible declares that in spite of our unworthiness, God loves us with an everlasting love. God wants you to receive His love by opening your heart to Him and letting Him show you how much He loves you.

God is waiting for you to give Him your burdens. He promises to take good care of you. God wants you to feel comfortable. The Bible tells us, "Give all your worries and cares to God, for he cares about you" (1 Peter 5:7 NLT).

Remember that the more you believe Jesus' words and obey God by faith, the more you will sing and jump with joy.

THE CRUCIFIXION AND RESURRECTION OF JESUS CHRIST

20

THE CRUCIFIXION OF
CHRIST ACCORDING
TO ISLAM

Some Muslims think that God would never have allowed the Jews to crucify Jesus, because He is honored in the Qur'an as a great prophet. I would like to remind these beloved Muslims of verses from the Qur'an that teach of *messengers* (prophets) of God who were killed:

> In that they [the Jews] broke their covenant; that they rejected the Signs of Allah; That they slew the messengers in defiance of right. (Surah 4:155)

> That whenever there comes to you [the Jews] a Messenger with what ye yourselves desire not, ye are puffed up with pride? Some ye called impostors, and others ye slay. (Surah 2:87) (Also see Surah 2:91 and Surah 3:183.)

I just thought about an interesting observation. Muslims and Christians agree that God's prophets represent God's feelings and thoughts. If we also agree that many of them suffered in the process of representing God and communicating God's message, then Muslim teachers should not think that it is strange that God, who sent the prophets, also suffered for our sake through the person of Jesus Christ.

I know that many Muslim teachers view a prophet killed at the hand of his enemies as a defeat. For this reason, I'd like to present to you this question: which of the following choices honors Jesus most and brings glory to God?

1. If Jesus used violence to attack the people who were trying to arrest Him,
2. If Jesus escaped, or
3. If Jesus took the worst His enemies could inflict on Him (death on the cross), then publicly conquered death by resurrecting from the dead.

Obviously this third action will bring the most glory to God, and it is exactly what the Bible declares that Jesus did.

THE QUR'AN'S VAGUE ACCOUNT OF JESUS' CRUCIFIXION

In the entire Qur'an, there is only one passage that mentions the crucifixion. Surah 4:157–158 states: "That they said (in boast), 'We killed Christ Jesus the son of Mary, The Messenger of Allah'—But they killed him not, nor crucified him, but so it was made to appear to them. . . . For of a surety they killed him not, Nay, Allah raised him up unto Himself."

The subject of this passage is not Jesus; it is actually the Jews.

This passage is not dealing with whether or not Jesus was killed, but rather with who killed Him.

To whom was the Qur'an referring when it said, "They killed him not, nor crucified him"? The answer from the context is, of course, the unbelieving Jews. The purpose of this verse is not to deny that Jesus was killed or crucified. It merely states that "they" (the Jews) did not kill or crucify Him. This verse denies the proud Jewish boast that they killed Jesus.

JESUS' CRUCIFIXION AND GOD'S MASTER PLAN OF SALVATION

The Gospel teaches that the crucifixion of Jesus was according to God's "deliberate plan and foreknowledge" (Acts 2:23). According to the Gospel account, Pilate claimed to have the power of life or death over Jesus. However, Jesus answered Pilate saying, "You would have no power over me if it were not given to you from above" (John 19:11).

Christians know and believe, based on the Bible, that God was the primary cause for Jesus' crucifixion. It is revealed throughout the Bible that Christ's coming, crucifixion, and resurrection were planned by God before the world began.

The Qur'an also states that God allowed Jesus to die and then raised Him up after His death (Surah 3:55).

"THE SUBSTITUTION THEORY"

Muslim scholars generally teach that Jesus was substituted when He faced arrest and death. They believe God changed the face of someone else, making that man look like Jesus. So when the Jews and Romans tried to arrest Jesus, they thought the substitute was Jesus and arrested and crucified him by mistake.

Most of the Muslim scholars believe that at the very moment of this substitution, God lifted Jesus up bodily into heaven. Note that the Muslim scholars are not in agreement as to the identity of the substituted person who supposedly replaced Jesus.

"The Substitution Theory" Challenged

The Muslim scholars base their belief in the substitution theory upon this one unclear verse that states: "but so it was made to appear to them" (Surah 4:157). Christian scholar E. E. Elder comments on this verse and clarifies:

> There is no mention of a substitute here, or anywhere else in the Qur'an. It seems obvious that "it" cannot refer to Jesus. It certainly must refer to something else that has been mentioned. Now the phrase could be translated, "it was made a misunderstanding—a perplexity to them." In that case the subject understood would refer to His crucifixion. The verse could then be properly translated, "yet they slew him not, and they crucified him not—but it (Jesus' crucifixion) was made a misunderstanding to them." His crucifixion perplexed them. They saw the event, but failed to appreciate its inner meaning. They even thought that they had power over his life.[1]

Therefore, it is not possible to reach a definitive conclusion based on this single and ambiguous verse in the Qur'an. One possible way to interpret Surah 4:157–158 is that the unbelieving Jews intended for the crucifixion of Jesus to shame Him in the eyes of the world. The ridicule He would suffer would then destroy Him in the hearts and eyes of the people. Also, His death would invalidate His mission. However, the Jews failed to accomplish that goal. On the contrary, by the crucifixion, the name and person of Jesus was glorified when God later raised Him up to be with Him.

Ironically, what Satan (through unbelieving Jews) used to kill Jesus, God the Father used to exalt the Christ. The Gospel notes that on the cross Jesus "disarmed the [evil] powers and authorities, he made a public spectacle of them, triumphing over them by the cross" (Colossians 2:15). Again, the crucifixion actually fulfilled God's plan. God won the victory by the cross by raising Jesus from the dead!

"The Substitution Theory" Examined

Not only is the Qur'an's teaching about the crucifixion brief and vague, but the substitution theory itself cannot be believed on moral and logical grounds for the following reasons:

- What kind of God would take a person and change his appearance to look like Jesus so that he would be subject to arrest and then crucifixion in place of Jesus? The substitution theory portrays God as guilty of misrepresenting one man as another, which is misleading and dishonest. We know that God does not lie.
- Why should anyone innocent of a capital crime suffer crucifixion? Why would God cause an innocent substitute person to be killed? God could have rescued Jesus without giving someone else to the Jews to crucify. The substitution theory is not consistent with the character of a loving, just, and merciful God.
- The Gospel records the words of Jesus while on the cross. All of the verses confirm that the person on the cross could only be Jesus. One example is Jesus' prayer for His enemies in Luke 23:34: "Father, forgive them, for they do

not know what they are doing." Can you imagine an innocent person hanging on the cross while having an attitude
of forgiveness toward those who were crucifying him?
Only the holy and humble Servant Jesus could do this!

- Based on the teachings of the Qur'an and the Bible about
the pure character of Christ, He would never permit another man—even Judas—to take His place on the
cross and suffer the consequences of His own teachings
and mission.

- What kind of God would cause Mary, the mother of
Jesus, and His beloved friends to suffer in such a way?
For they stood at the cross watching the agony of the one
whom they thought to be Jesus (John 19:25–27). Would
God cause His followers to go through this torturous
experience because of an illusion that He Himself
had orchestrated?

- Is it reasonable to believe that the faithful and true God
would mislead Jesus' devoted disciples by casting Jesus'
likeness upon someone else, making another man look
like Jesus? It is because the man who hung and died on the
cross looked exactly like Jesus that the disciples of Jesus
believed and proclaimed Jesus' crucifixion and death.

- More than two billion people today all over the world base
their faith on the historicity of the crucifixion and the
resurrection of Jesus!

My Muslim friend, is it logical to believe that God would
allow the foundation of the Christian faith to be based on a mis-
identification that God Himself orchestrated? Such a theory
would make God the author of the biggest hoax in human history. This cannot be. By nature, He is a just and holy God who
does only what is right! (1 Peter 1:15).

ISLAM DOES NOT DENY THE CRUCIFIXION

I ask you, my friend, to please recognize that Islam *does not entirely* deny the story of the crucifixion, as people usually think. According to the teachings of the Muslim scholars:

- Islam accepts that the Jews plotted to crucify Jesus.
- Islam accepts that Jesus was present on a certain day and that the Jews were seeking to arrest Him.
- Islam accepts that Jesus remained unwavering in loyalty to His mission. He did not escape and was ready to face His arrest.
- Islam accepts that the man arrested appeared to the Jews to look exactly like Jesus, and that the man who died on the cross looked exactly like Jesus. Everyone present at the cross recognized him to be Jesus.

Significantly, the only part of the crucifixion event that most Muslim scholars deny is that the person who died on the cross was actually Jesus!

Various Muslim Beliefs Concerning Jesus' Death

In view of Surah 4:157–158, the majority of the Muslim scholars believe Jesus did not die at all, but that God lifted Him up bodily into heaven—that He ascended alive to heaven. They believe this is how His life on earth ended.

On the other hand, well-regarded Muslim scholars disagree. They point out Surahs in the Qur'an that record Jesus' death. One such passage is Surah 19:33, which clearly records the death of Jesus. In this passage, Jesus is quoted as saying, "So peace is on me the day I was born, the day that I die, and the day that I shall be raised up to life (again)." Clearly these are successive days: The day of birth, the day of His death, and the day He shall be resurrected. According to the interpretation of these Muslim scholars, this verse reveals that Jesus died prior to being brought back to life.

Two contradicting Muslim views exist. While the Qur'an clearly mentions the death of Jesus, most Muslim scholars, based on Surah 4:157–158, believe that He ascended into heaven without dying at all. Some Muslim scholars, in an attempt to reconcile these views, teach that Christ will come back to this world someday to do many great and wonderful things, and then He will die.

The evidence disproving this teaching is Surah 19:33, which does not describe the sequence of Jesus' life as first, birth ("The day I was born"); second, resurrection ("The day I shall be raised up"); third, death ("The day that I die").

Nowhere does the Qur'an state that Jesus is yet to die!

Other verses in the Qur'an that discuss the death of Jesus use the past tense, indicating it has already happened.

For example, we read an identical passage in Surah 19:15 about Yahya (John the Baptist): "So peace on him the day he was born, the day that he dies, and the day that he will be raised up to life (again)!"

It is a recognized fact that Yahya died and was buried. And the reference to being "raised to life again" refers to the day of resurrection. Abdullah Yusuf Ali comments on this passage: "This is spoken as in the lifetime of Yahya. Peace and Allah's Blessings were on him when he was born; they continue when he is about to die an unjust death at the hands of the tyrant; and they will be especially manifest at the Day of Judgement."[2] Therefore, according to the meaning of the parallel verse, Jesus likewise died.

Muslim scholar A. H. Obaray also comments on Surah 19:33. He believes Jesus did die and He will not return to die. He writes: "No Muslim will shift the death of John to the future. All know that John died. . . . Since no one can now shift the death of John to the future, therefore no one can now shift the death of Jesus to the future. In fact there is not one single passage throughout the Qur'an showing that Jesus will return to die. The parallel statement with regard to John, who died, clearly shows that Jesus also died."[3]

Other such passages that speak of the death of Jesus include Surah 3:55 and Surah 5:117, which states "when thou didst take me up." Other translations of this verse in the Qur'an read: "take me to thyself" and "cause me to die" (*tawaffaitani*).

The expression *tawaffaitani* is explained by Dr. Mahmud Shaltut, one of the previous presidents of Al Azhar University:[4] "(It) is entitled in this verse to bear the meaning of ordinary death. . . . There is no way to interpret 'death' as occurring after his return from heaven . . . because the verse very clearly limits the connection of Jesus . . . to his own people of his own day and the connection is not with the people living at the time when he returns."[5]

Many Muslim scholars continue to struggle with these verses that refer to the death of Jesus.

Various Muslim Theories Concerning Jesus' Death

Abdullah Yusuf Ali commented on Surah 4:157, which states: "But they killed him not, nor crucified him." Ali said, "The end of the life of Jesus on earth is as much involved in *mystery* as his birth."[6] And regarding Surah 4:158, which states: "Nay, Allah raised him up unto himself," Ali writes:

There is difference of opinion as to the exact interpretation of this verse. The words are: The Jews did not kill Jesus, but Allah raised him up to Himself. One school holds that Jesus did not die the usual human death, but still lives in the body in heaven, which is the generally accepted Muslim view. Another holds that he did die but not when he was supposed to be crucified, and that his being "raised up" unto Allah means that instead of being disgraced as a malefactor, as the Jews intended, he was on the contrary honored by Allah as His Messenger.[7]

Distinguished Muslim scholars and commentators such as Zamakshari, Ibn Abbas, and others state that Christ remained dead for several hours before being raised to heaven. In addition, Al-Razi records that some Muslim theologians believe Jesus was dead for three hours and others say seven hours.[8]

Maududi, a renowned modern Muslim scholar in Pakistan, comments on Surah 4:157: "After this, God who can do any and everything He wills, raised Jesus to Himself and rescued him from crucifixion and the one who was crucified afterwards was somehow or other taken for Christ."[9] Note the vagueness in his statement.

Daryabadi, another noted Pakastani Muslim theologian says, "It was not Jesus who was executed but another, who was miraculously substituted (how and in what way is another question, and is not touched upon in the Qur'an) for him."[10] This statement regarding the crucifixion also is obscure.

The Qur'an Does Not Disqualify the Biblical Account

Because of the vague, limited, and apparently contradictory verses in the Qur'an, Muslim scholars are unsure about the end of the life of Jesus on earth. They disagree about whether He died on earth then raised to heaven, or was raised alive to heaven without dying at all. Since these scholars have no definitive evidence or specific information regarding the circumstances of the crucifixion, their differing conclusions involve speculation and theory.

My dear reader, since there is confusion among Muslim scholars about Jesus' death, Islam does allow for the possibility that the biblical account is accurate. As previously stated, the

Qur'an does recognize the Bible as the primary source of enlightenment, as clearly indicated in Surah 10:94, which states, "If thou [Muhammad] wert in doubt as to what we have revealed unto thee then ask those who have been reading the Book from before thee." This verse clearly instructs all the Muslim believers to refer to the Bible when questions arise regarding the Qur'an's meaning. Now let us go to the next chapter and examine the biblical account of Jesus' crucifixion and resurrection.

21

THE CRUCIFIXION AND RESURRECTION OF JESUS ACCORDING TO THE GOSPEL

A ll of the accounts in the Gospel are specific and consistent that Christ was crucified, He died, and He rose from the dead.

FOUNDATIONAL FAITH OF FOLLOWERS OF CHRIST

For nearly two thousand years, all true followers of Christ throughout the world have believed in the crucifixion, death, and resurrection of Jesus Christ because of the clear testimonies in the Bible to these facts.

We can trust the Bible and what it says about Jesus' crucifixion because it records the testimony of eyewitnesses. The Bible records what took place in public.

For example, the apostle Peter, speaking to the Jews after the healing of a crippled man, boldly stated, "Then know this, you and all the people of Israel: It is by the name of Jesus Christ of Nazareth, whom you crucified but whom God raised from the dead, that this man stands before you healed" (Acts 4:10).

Seven weeks after Jesus' crucifixion, Peter said to a great multitude of Jews:

> "Fellow Israelites, listen to this: Jesus of Nazareth was a man accredited by God to you by miracles, wonders and signs, which God did among you through him, as you yourselves know. This man was handed over to you by God's deliberate plan and foreknowledge; and you, with the help of wicked men, put him to death by nailing him to the cross. But God raised him from the dead, freeing him from the agony of death, because it was impossible for death to keep its hold on him." (Acts 2:22–24)

When Peter said these words to the Jews who were there, they never denied that they crucified Jesus. The Bible records that three thousand of them put their faith in Jesus after Peter finished speaking to them. Would they have believed in Jesus if they had any doubt that He was really crucified?

And in the Gospel, Jesus predicts His own death and resurrection to His twelve disciples:

> Jesus took the Twelve aside and told them, "We are going up to Jerusalem, and everything that is written by the prophets about the Son of Man will be fulfilled. He will be delivered over to the Gentiles. They will mock him, insult him and spit on him; they will flog him and kill him. On the third day he will rise again." (Luke 18:31–33; see also John 2:19–21)

OLD TESTAMENT PROPHECIES
REGARDING JESUS' CRUCIFIXION

The New Testament was written after the crucifixion and contains details of it; the Old Testament was written hundreds of years before the crucifixion and contains amazing prophecies about it. Two of these amazing specific prophecies are found in Isaiah 53 and Psalm 22.

Jesus' Death and Burial

Isaiah 53:9 gives specific details about the death of Jesus hundreds of years before He was even born: "He was assigned a grave with the wicked, and with the rich in his death." No one at the time of the prophet Isaiah could understand the meaning of these words. The account of His burial appeared to be a contradiction. Was Jesus buried with the outcasts or was He buried with the noble and rich?

Both seemingly contradictory statements regarding Jesus' burial in Isaiah 53:9 came to pass. First of all, Jesus "was assigned a grave with the wicked" because He was crucified between two thieves, fulfilling the first part of the prophecy. Criminals who were crucified were often assigned to be thrown into a burning pit and cremated. However, this did not happen to Jesus.

The second half of this prophecy was fulfilled when Jesus was buried in the tomb of Joseph, a rich man. Matthew 27:57–60 reads:

As evening approached, there came a rich man from Arimathea, named Joseph, who had himself become a disciple of Jesus. Going to Pilate, he asked for Jesus' body, and Pilate ordered that it be given to him. Joseph took the body, wrapped it in a clean linen cloth, and placed it in his own new tomb that he had cut out of the rock.

By being crucified with thieves and buried in the tomb of a rich man, Jesus was assigned a grave with both the wicked and the rich. Thus, what seemed an unexplained paradox in Isaiah 53 was easily understood when Jesus came and fulfilled the prophecy!

The Dividing of Christ's Clothes

Other prophetic words of Christ's crucifixion are found in Psalm 22:18: "They divide My garments among them, and for My clothing they cast lots" (NKJV). This verse was a mystery to the people at that time and seemed to contain another contradiction. Did they take the clothes and divide them among themselves, or did they cast lots to see who would get them? Which one was it?

The fulfillment of this prophecy is documented in John 19:23–24. When the soldiers crucified Jesus, they took His clothes and divided them into four shares, one for each of them. This fulfilled the first part of the prophecy: "They divide my garments among them." But the undergarment remained. It was seamless and woven in one piece from top to bottom. The soldiers said to one another, "Let's not tear it, let's decide by lot who will get it." By doing this, the soldiers fulfilled the second part of the prophecy that said, "They cast lots for my clothing." The prophecy of Psalm 22:18 was explained and fulfilled to the letter at the foot of the cross.

Incidentally, the Jews in the first century who rejected Jesus as their Savior dared not delete from their sacred Scripture any one of the numerous Messianic prophecies that were fulfilled in Jesus. If they did not delete Scripture at this crucial time in their religious history, how could they be suspected of altering it six hundred years later when Islam appeared on the scene?

Historicity of the Crucifixion

The crucifixion of Jesus is a well-attested event in history. Modern historians agree that Jesus was a historical character and that He was crucified. Even one of the most acclaimed Muslim writers in the history of Egypt, Abaas Mahmood Al Akad (who lived in the nineteenth century), wrote a book about the life of Christ, in which he confirmed that we can depend on the four Gospels (the books of Matthew, Mark, Luke, and John) as historical evidence to know what happened in Jesus' life.[1]

Jesus' death is directly mentioned more than 150 times in the New Testament. For example, see Matthew 27:50, John 19:30, 33–35, and Luke 23:46.

Again, it is not rational to believe the claim, made more than six hundred years after Christ's crucifixion, that the person crucified was not Christ but rather someone else who looked exactly like Him. An analogy would be if a man were to come hundreds of years from now and tell the world that the person assassinated in America in the twentieth century was not Martin Luther King Jr. himself, but rather someone who looked exactly like him.

Furthermore, if the biblical and other historic records of the crucifixion had been untrue, we would expect the Qur'an to have many verses stating that Jesus did not die on the cross. However, the amazing truth is that in more than six thousand Qur'anic verses there is not a single one that clearly refutes Jesus' crucifixion. Not one verse indicates that the Gospel was incorrect on this point.

JESUS, A PERFECT EXAMPLE
OF SURRENDER AND SUBMISSION

The word "Muslim" means one who surrenders and submits. If you want to know what a man looks like who is absolutely submitted to God, look to Jesus. Jesus was a perfect man. His crucifixion actually demonstrates the meaning of the word "Muslim."

Jesus obeyed God the Father to the end. Note that Jesus submitted Himself to the will of His Father (leading Him to the cross to be sacrificed), just as Abraham's son submitted himself to the will of his father (leading him to the altar to be sacrificed). The crucifixion of Jesus represents the ultimate surrender to the will of God! Jesus said, "I have come down from heaven not to do my will but to do the will of him who sent me" (John 6:38).

With humility, we as followers of Christ view the crucifixion as the reason for giving the greatest honor to Jesus, who willingly took our place and punishment on the cross (Hebrews 12:2). We also stand in awe at the power of God in raising Jesus from the dead and accomplishing our salvation!

Jesus taught His followers what true submission to God really is. For example, Jesus taught us to pray that God's kingdom come and God's will be done here on earth as it is done in heaven (Matthew 6:10). Jesus taught us not to live for ourselves, but to live to please God.

JESUS CAME BACK FROM THE DEAD!

Jesus' disciples believed in His resurrection because they actually saw Him alive after His death by crucifixion. One account of Jesus' resurrection is found in the following passage:

> The angel said to the women, "Do not be afraid, for I know that you are looking for Jesus, who was crucified. He is not here; he has risen, just as he said. Come and see the place where he lay. Then go quickly and tell his disciples: 'He has risen from the dead and is going ahead of you into Galilee. There you will see him.' Now I have told you." (Matthew 28:5–7)

The resurrection refers to the return of Christ to bodily life on earth on the third day after His death. Jesus' body, which had been buried, was resurrected as a glorified body.

Jesus Appears to His Disciples

We read in the Bible: "When the disciples were together, with the doors locked for fear of the Jewish leaders, Jesus came and stood among them and said, 'Peace be with you.' After he said this, he showed them his hands and side. The disciples were overjoyed when they saw the Lord" (John 20:19–20).

Jesus Christ showed Himself to His disciples that they might see that He resurrected from the dead. Christ showed His disciples His hands and side that still had the marks and wounds of the cross in order that they know for sure that this man before them truly was Jesus who had been crucified. Jesus gave them unquestionable proof of His identity.

After Jesus rose from the dead, he personally spoke to Thomas who was doubting His resurrection, and said to him, "Put your finger here; see my hands. Reach out your hand and put it into my side. Stop doubting and believe" (John 20:27).

Because Thomas saw the physically resurrected Christ, he was inspired and compelled to preach the gospel even in India. Tradition holds that wherever he went he spoke about Jesus' death and resurrection. Thomas became a martyr because of this message that he proclaimed.

Hundreds of witnesses saw the risen Christ over a forty-day period in various locations and at various times. For example, Jesus was seen in His resurrected body by more than five hundred brethren at once (1 Corinthians 15:1–6). Please see other accounts of Jesus' resurrection in John 21:1–23, Mark 16:9–13, and Acts 1:3.

When you read John 20, you will know that there were eye-witnesses that Jesus' tomb was empty. The resurrection proclamation could not have been believed in Jerusalem if the emptiness of the tomb had not been established. Please read the testimony about Jesus that the apostle Peter recorded in Acts 10:38–43.

The Holy Scriptures Foretold Jesus' Resurrection

God inspired David (Daud) to predict the resurrection of the Christ: "Therefore my heart is glad, and my glory rejoices; My flesh also will rest in hope. For You will not leave my soul in Sheol, nor will You allow Your Holy One to see corruption" (Psalm 16:9–10 NKJV).

The apostle Peter applied this prophecy to the resurrection of Jesus when he said to the Jews:

> David said about [Jesus]: ". . . because you will not abandon me to the realm of the dead, you will not let your holy one see decay. . . ."
>
> "Fellow Israelites, I can tell you confidently that the patriarch David died and was buried, and his tomb is here to this day. But he was a prophet and knew that God had promised him on oath that he would place one of his descendants on his throne. Seeing what was to come, he spoke of the resurrection of the Messiah, that he was not abandoned to the realm of the dead, nor did his body see decay. God has raised this Jesus to life, and we are all witnesses of it." (Acts 2:25, 27–32)

Two Credible Professors Speak Out on Historical Evidence

Professor Thomas Arnold, the Lord Master of Rugby University, author of *The History of Rome* and the holder of the Chair of Modern History at Oxford University, was well equipped to evaluate evidence to determine historical fact. After carefully sifting the ancient documentation for the crucifixion and resurrection of Christ, this renowned, modern-day scholar wrote:

I have been used for many years to study the histories of other times and to examine and weigh the evidence of those who have written about them. I know of no one fact in the history of mankind which is proven by better and fuller evidence of every sort, to the understanding of a fair inquirer, than the great sign which God has given us that Christ died and rose again from the dead.[2]

John Singleton Copley, a professor at Cambridge University and Attorney General of Great Britain in 1824, rose to the highest office as judge in England. He was recognized as one of the greatest legal minds in British history. After his death, a document was found among his private papers in which he had written: "I know pretty well what evidence is and I tell you, such evidence as that for the resurrection has never been broken down yet."[3]

Historicity of the Resurrection

Note that certain facts are undisputed even by secular (non-religious) historians and they include:

- Jesus Christ was crucified and died.
- Jesus' tomb was empty after His burial (John 20).
- There was a proclamation that Jesus had risen.

According to the Gospel, after Jesus Christ died by crucifixion, one of the soldiers pierced His side with a spear (John 19:34). Then His body was taken down from the cross and laid in the tomb of Joseph of Arimathea. A large and heavy stone was placed at the front of the tomb, and the Roman seal was placed on that stone. Well-trained Roman guards constantly watched and guarded the tomb. On the third day, the tomb was empty.

Following Jesus' arrest, His disciples were afraid. We read:

"Then all the disciples deserted him and fled" (Matthew 26:56). However, several days after the resurrection, this same group became courageous. Their transformation occurred not only because they had seen an empty tomb, but because they had seen and experienced the risen Christ.

Credibility of Jesus' Disciples

If someone were to ask, "Did the disciples lie about seeing Jesus alive again?" the answer would be simple. What could they possibly have gained by lying? Prestige? Wealth? According to tradition, Jude and Simon Peter were crucified; Luke was hanged from an olive tree; Paul was beheaded; Philip was scourged and crucified; James (son of Zebedee) was killed by the sword; Mark was dragged through the streets by his feet and then burned alive; James (half brother of Jesus) and Barnabas were stoned to death. This treatment was their earthly "reward" for proclaiming the good news:

Jesus is risen, He is alive, He offers forgiveness of sins, and He gives eternal life to those who believe in Him!

Would these disciples subject themselves to such cruel punishment if they had any doubt that Jesus rose from the dead? Let me answer that with this observation. When I was a lawyer in Egypt, I worked for my father who has practiced law for about fifty years. Likewise, my grandfather was also a lawyer for about fifty years. My older brother, Farid, used to work as the chief judge of the Supreme Court in Egypt. He retired in August 2014. Most of my extended family is in the legal profession. We have never seen or heard of a witness who allowed himself to go to prison or to suffer for something that he knew was a lie.

THE ASCENSION AND RETURN OF JESUS CHRIST

22

THE ASCENSION OF JESUS

Islam clearly teaches that Jesus was lifted up to be with God and is alive today. For example, Surah 4:158 states: "Allah raised him unto Himself."

In addition, there are many Hadiths supporting the ascension of Jesus. Generally, the Muslim world believes that God lifted up Jesus bodily into heaven and that He went up alive to heaven.

The Gospel records the ascension of Jesus in Mark 16:19: "After the Lord Jesus had spoken to them [His apostles], he was taken up into heaven." See His ascension accounts also in Luke 24:49–53 and Acts 1:9–11.

We see that both the Qur'an and the Bible teach that Jesus ascended not just into heaven, but indeed into the ultimate presence of God. The Qur'an and the Bible agree on the fact that Jesus Christ is alive in heaven to this day.

PURPOSE OF THE ASCENSION
OFFERED BY MUSLIM SCHOLARS

Many Muslim scholars claim that God raised Jesus to Himself in order to save Him from crucifixion by the Jews.

It is difficult to accept the theory that "God took Jesus up to Himself" (in Surah 4:158) just as an escape route to rescue Him from the hands of the Jews. First of all, God could have used a less dramatic way to deliver Jesus. An example is in the Gospel according to Matthew 2:13: When Herod wanted to kill Jesus, an angel warned Joseph in a dream and told him to take the child and His mother and flee to Egypt.

Furthermore, Jesus could have saved Himself from the hands of the Jews. For according to the Bible (and the Qur'an agrees):

- Jesus had the ability to know the unseen (Matthew 16:21; cf. Surah 3:49).
- Jesus had the ability to perform miracles (Matthew 4:23; cf. Surah 5:110).

THE BIBLE EXPLAINS THE REASON FOR JESUS' ASCENSION

According to the Gospel, Jesus is the eternal Son of God, and heaven is His permanent home. Therefore, it was impossible for Him, after He accomplished His mission on earth, to return to dust like all other prophets and men naturally do. Rather, He returned to heaven from where He came. Jesus said, "For I have come down from heaven not to do my will but to do the will of him who sent me" (John 6:38).

In John 8:23, we read that Jesus told the Jews, "You are from below; I am from above. You are of this world; I am not of this world."

The Eternal Son of God Returned to Heaven

Remember, my dear Muslim reader, the Qur'an said in Surah 4:171 that Jesus is a "Spirit proceeding from God." It seems fitting then that only He who came from God could go back to be with God.

According to the Bible, after Jesus died and completed His work on the cross, He was reunited with God the Father. The ascension of Christ meant the end of His earthly ministry and the beginning of His heavenly ministry. It also meant that God accepted Jesus' service and sacrifice on our behalf.

My dear friend, Jesus Christ is, without a doubt, higher than all creation. He is alive with the heavenly Father today! It is amazing, my dear reader! Jesus' divine nature makes Him at home with the majesty and holiness of God the Father.

23

THE SECOND COMING OF JESUS

While Islam and Christianity differ on the details, both acknowledge that Jesus is coming back to earth. This event is referred to as the "second coming of Jesus."

THE QUR'AN AND THE BIBLE REFER TO JESUS' SECOND COMING

In the Qur'an, Surah 43:61 states: "He (*Jesus*) is, in fact, a sign for the coming of the Hour of Doom" (Muhammad Farooq-I-Azam Malik). Abdullah Yusuf Ali commented on this verse in his translation of the Qur'an: "This is understood to refer to the second coming of Jesus in the Last Days before the resurrection when he will destroy the false doctrines that pass under his name."[1]

Throughout the centuries, most Muslim commentators have interpreted Surah 43:61 as a prophecy of Jesus' second coming.

It is interesting, my dear Muslim friend, that this event is prophesied in the Old Testament (Daniel 7:13–14).

This passage in Daniel is a clear prophecy of the second coming of Jesus Christ that is confirmed in the Gospel in Mark 13:26, which reads: "At that time people will see the Son of Man coming in clouds with great power and glory."

According to Muslim theologians, Jesus will return from heaven, heralding the climax of human history, and will assume control over the whole world. Jesus alone is to herald the hour of judgment. Ibn-Atya, a distinguished Muslim commentator, states that "Muslim theologians are unanimous in contending that Jesus Christ is physically alive at present in heaven and is destined to return to this world . . . towards the approach of the Last Day."[2]

Certainly the Hadith teaches that Jesus will return from heaven in the last days. There are approximately seventy Traditions in support of the doctrine of the return of Jesus to earth. All of them are considered to be of unquestioned reliability.

WHO IS THE JUDGE?

The Qur'an states clearly that God controls the day of judgment. "In the name of Allah . . . Master of the Day of Judgment" (Surah 1:1, 4).

Significantly, Muhammad said, "Surely (Jesus), the son of Mary will soon descend among you and will judge mankind justly (as a just ruler)."[3] Now, who exactly is this "man" who can judge every person justly? Don't you wonder, my friend? Jesus said, "For the Son of Man will come with his angels in the glory of his Father and will judge all people according to their deeds" (Matthew 16:27 NLT).

Jesus Is Going to Judge the World

The Bible teaches that the Son of God, by coming in the likeness of man, has revealed God to men and has brought men face-to-face with God. He shall return to judge the earth. Jesus Himself declares, "Moreover, the Father judges no one, but has entrusted all judgment to the Son, that all may honor the Son just as they honor the Father. Whoever does not honor the Son does not honor the Father, who sent him" (John 5:22–23).

Jesus goes on to say, "For as the Father has life in himself, so he has granted the Son also to have life in himself. And he has given him authority to judge because he is the Son of Man" (John 5:26–27).

When Jesus comes back to earth, He will be shining with all the brightness of His heavenly glory. A glimpse of Jesus' divine glory is recorded in the Gospel account of Matthew when He was momentarily *transfigured* on earth. On a high mountain (before three of His disciples), Jesus' "face shown like the sun, and his clothes became as white as the light" (Matthew 17:1–13). In harmony with this revelation, Suyuti comments on Surah 6:158: "Then the earth will shine with the light of its Lord and Jesus, Son of Mary, will descend." Jesus will appear from heaven in power and glory.

Jesus will be the most glorious sight that humans have ever seen. The Suffering Servant will come back as the Conquering King. He will put an end to evil and will rule with holy justice!

True Believers Will Be Transformed into Jesus' Image

When Jesus comes back, He will transform His true fol-lowers (true believers) into His image, to share His glory with them forever. We read about this glorious promise in the Gospel: "But our citizenship is in heaven. And we eagerly await a Savior from there, the Lord Jesus Christ, who, by the power that enables him to bring everything under his control, will transform our lowly bodies so that they will be like his glorious body" (Philippians 3:20–21).

Jesus will give us new, glorified bodies suited for heaven. At Jesus' first coming He made Himself like us, but at Jesus' second coming He will make us like Him. We read this awesome news in the Bible:

> We know that when Christ appears, we shall be like him, for we shall see him as he is. (1 John 3:2)

Jesus Will Take Believers to Heaven to Be with Him

My dear Muslim friend, the purpose of Jesus' coming into our world was to save us and give us eternal life. Part of the good news of the Bible is that when Jesus descends from heaven, He will gather all people who believe in Him. Then we will join Him, "and so we will be with the Lord forever" (1 Thessalonians 4:17)!

We look forward to this glorious day when we will be with Jesus. He has promised us:

> Don't let your hearts be troubled. Trust in God, and trust also in me. There is more than enough room in my Father's home. If this were not so, would I have told you that I am going to prepare a place for you? When everything is ready, I will come and get you, so that you will always be with me where I am. (John 14:1–3 NLT)

Islam Teaches That Jesus Alone Will Defeat the False Christ

According to the Hadith, a false christ (*Dajjal*) will appear before the Hour of Doom. The Dajjal (which means "the deceiver" in Arabic) will pretend he is the Christ. (Note that the Bible identifies this individual as the Antichrist.) He will perform many miracles. According to the Hadith, the false christ will be the ultimate manifestation of evil. He will cause the greatest assault against the only true God. He will attempt to cause the greatest harm to mankind.

Muhammad said, "There would be no creation (creating more trouble) than the Dajjal right from The creation of Adam to the Last Hour."[4] We read in one of the Hadiths that Muhammad frequently prayed, "O Allah! I seek refuge with you from the punishment in the grave and from the punishment in The Hell fire and from the afflictions of life and death, and the afflictions of Al-Masih Ad-Dajjal."[5]

In the Hadith, it is recorded that Ayisha said: "I heard Allah's Apostle [Muhammad] in his prayer seeking refuge with Allah from the affliction of Al-Masih Ad-Dajjal."[6] Also in the Hadith, Christ (Isa) is the only One whom God will send to defeat the false christ, save mankind, restore faith in the true God, and establish peace on earth!

According to the Hadith, Muhammad said, "Jesus, Son of Mary, will descend . . . and will lead them in prayer. When the enemy of Allah (the Dajjal) sees him, he will dissolve just as salt dissolves in water."[7] His statement is very thought provoking, my dear reader! Only Jesus will win the most tremendous and final battle in the history of humanity.

Muhammad also stated: "Then a people whom Allah had protected would come to Jesus, Son of Mary, and he would wipe their faces and would inform them of their ranks in Paradise."[8] How amazing! Who is this man who is supposed to tell people their condition in paradise before the day of judgment?

Regarding the Dajjal, Muhammad said, "I warn you of him and there is no prophet who has not warned his people against the Dajjal."[9] Isn't it interesting, my dear Muslim reader, that according to Muhammad, every prophet came to warn his nation of the deception of the Dajjal, but Christ alone is supposed to come again to earth to destroy the *false christ* without even the assistance of an angel or a prophet?

24

THE UNIQUENESS OF JESUS COMPELS A CONCLUSION

My dear Muslim friend, I hope you will continue to ask God to guide you to the straight path that leads to Him. God desires us to be sincere in evaluating and accepting the truth He reveals to us.

JESUS, MORE THAN A MERE PROPHET

While Muhammad perceived Jesus Christ only as a prophet, the Qur'an and the Bible attribute to Him characteristics that only belong to God. The unique features of Jesus' life prove that He is more than a mere prophet. The prophets we have heard or read about were ordinary men. Each one was born of a father and a mother. They lived a normal life. Sometimes they did good things and other times they sinned against God and against fellow human beings. When their lives ended, they returned to the dust from where they came.

Consider again that both the Qur'an and the Gospel attribute three similar titles to Jesus that are consistent with the Christian belief that Jesus is Lord and Savior. These divine titles are: the *Word of God*, *Messiah*, and *Spirit from God*.

We learn from the Qur'an and the Bible that Jesus' life was unique. He was set apart even before conception. Jesus' virgin birth tells us that God made the only exception to the natural process of procreation, in having Jesus conceived by the power of God's Spirit. Jesus was also unique in His sinlessness, His ability to raise the dead, perform the greatest miracles, His ascension, and His inevitable return to judge the world. Thus, His abilities, titles, and traits are collective evidence that compel the conclusion that Jesus is more than just a prophet.

There is considerable commonality between the Bible and the Qur'an regarding the person of Jesus Christ (AL-Masih, Isa). When you examine the parallels within them, God certainly will guide you to the complete truth.

THE GLORIOUS AND SUPERNATURAL PERSON OF JESUS

My beloved Muslim friend, please ask yourself, why were all these unique and heavenly features found only in Jesus Christ?

Jesus' uniqueness is totally the result of the will and power of God. It was God who gave Jesus an exceptional life on earth.

When you prayerfully consider the unique features in Jesus' life, you will certainly discover that there is something majestic and heavenly about the Man Jesus. There is something particularly glorious and supernatural about the Person of Jesus! The idea that Jesus Christ was merely a prophet and messenger surely is unreasonable in the light of the evidence surrounding His life.

As you prayerfully ponder and evaluate all the facts about Jesus presented in this book, you will discover that Jesus' uniqueness demands the conclusion that Jesus is the unique, eternal Son of God who came to save us.

Jesus was born and raised in a small village. He worked as a carpenter until He was thirty. He never had a position in government. He had no money and never owned a house. He never had an army. He never fought a war or commanded His disciples to fight. He ministered only for three and a half years and then His enemies arrested Him and crucified Him.

There has never been a prophet, a military leader, an educator, or a king who has made a more positive impact on humanity than Jesus. Jesus Christ is superior to all others in His moral influence and in His promotion of human welfare.

Jesus was unique and superior in His teaching. For example, He taught:

"Love your enemies." (Matthew 5:44)
"Love your neighbor as yourself." (Matthew 22:39)
"Bless those who curse you, pray for those who mistreat you." (Luke 6:28)

Humans are indeed weak, but God can enable us to live and grow closer and closer to His highest moral standard.

If you read Jesus' teachings recorded in the Bible, you will discover that if people only obeyed what Jesus taught, all the problems in the world would be solved.

Two thousand years have passed since the death of Jesus, and He is still the most loved and honored person who ever lived. My precious reader, by the time you have finished reading this book you will discover that Jesus is unique and had a superior, positive impact on humanity because of who He is and because God sent Him to rescue us.

All these unique features in Jesus' life find their very meaning and significance in two essential doctrines of Christianity: First, Jesus is the eternal and unique Son of God. Second, Jesus is the Savior of mankind. After discovering the divine uniqueness of Jesus Christ, you can invite Him into your life as Savior and receive the free gift of eternal life!

THE MYTH OF THE THREE GODS OF CHRISTIANITY

25

DO CHRISTIANS WORSHIP THREE GODS?

The Bible consistently reveals, in at least twenty-eight verses, that there is only one God (Tawhid). Jesus Christ Himself quotes the famous passage in the Torah, Deuteronomy 6:4–5: "Hear, O Israel: The Lord our God, the Lord is one. Love the Lord your God with all your heart and with all your soul and with all your mind and with all your strength" (Mark 12:29–30).

THE BIBLE TEACHES THERE IS ONLY ONE GOD

Numerous explicit statements in the Old and New Testaments declare that there is only one God of the entire universe. The Bible emphasizes monotheism and that God is one.

Old Testament examples include:

Deuteronomy 4:35, 39; 2 Samuel 7:22; 1 Kings 8:60; Isaiah 43:10–11; 45:5–6

New Testament examples include:

Romans 3:30; 1 Corinthians 8:4; Ephesians 4:6; Jude 25

GOD IS ONE ESSENCE
REVEALED IN THREE PERSONS

The Gospel recorded words Christ spoke to His disciples before He ascended:

"Therefore go and make disciples of all nations, baptizing them in the name of the Father and of the Son and of the Holy Spirit, and teaching them to obey everything I have commanded you. And surely I am with you always, to the very end of the age." (Matthew 28:19–20)

This passage refers to the tri-unity of the one God. Note that Jesus used "in the name" (singular) not "in the names" (plural). Throughout the Gospel, the Son and the Holy Spirit are not associates or partners with God, but rather the three Persons constitute only one God.

My dear reader, it is important to know that it is important Jesus proclaimed the truth of the Trinity. Jesus' disciples and the early church arrived to faith in the triune God as an understanding of what Jesus Christ had revealed.

Jesus talked about the Holy Spirit and told His disciples: "And I will ask the Father, and he will give you another advocate to help you and be with you forever—the Spirit of truth. The world cannot accept him, because it neither sees him nor knows him. But you know him, for he lives with you and will be in you" (John 14:16–17). Jesus also told them:

"The Advocate, the Holy Spirit, whom the Father will send in my name, will teach you all things and will remind you of everything I have said to you." (John 14:26)

"When the Advocate comes, whom I will send to you from the Father—the Spirit of truth who goes out from the Father—he will testify about me." (John 15:26)

"But very truly I tell you, it is for your good that I am going away. Unless I go away, the Advocate will not come to you; but if I go, I will send him to you. When he comes, he will prove the world to be in the wrong about sin . . ." (John 16:7–8)

"I have much more to say to you, more than you can now bear. But when he, the Spirit of truth, comes, he will guide you into all the truth. He will not speak on his own; he will speak only what he hears, and he will tell you what is yet to come. He will glorify me because it is from me that he will receive what he will make known to you. All that belongs to the Father is mine." (John 16:12–15a)

It is also clear throughout the Gospel that Jesus talked about Himself as the Son of God and of God as His Father. Jesus also said, "All things have been committed to me by my Father. No one knows the Son except the Father, and no one knows the Father except the Son and those to whom the Son chooses to reveal him" (Matthew 11:27). Again, this statement would be blasphemy if Jesus were just a human being.

Jesus claimed absolute equality with the Father when He said:

"I and the Father are one."

Again his Jewish opponents picked up stones to stone

215

Him, but Jesus said to them, "I have shown you many good works from the Father. For which of these do you stone me?"

"We are not stoning you for any good work," they replied, "but for blasphemy, because you, a mere man, claim to be God." (John 10:30–33)

The Old Testament Reveals the Tri-unity of God

The Old Testament contains a clear emphasis on God's oneness and unity as an emphatic declaration to the pagan nations surrounding the people of Israel (Deuteronomy 4:35).

The Old Testament also contains some references to the persons of the tri-unity. Regarding the Son, see Isaiah 7:14. Examples of references to the Holy Spirit are found in Genesis 1:2 and Nehemiah 9:20.

The New Testament Reveals the Tri-unity of God

The New Testament emphatically revealed the triune God to us and made this doctrine crystal clear. A tri-unity of Father, Son, and Holy Spirit is consistently presented throughout the New Testament. For example:

For through him [Jesus Christ] we both have access to the Father by one Spirit [Holy Spirit]. (Ephesians 2:18)

May the grace of the Lord Jesus Christ, and the love of God, and the fellowship of the Holy Spirit be with you all. (2 Corinthians 13:14)

God the Father knew you and chose you long ago, and his Spirit has made you holy. As a result, you have obeyed him and have been cleansed by the blood of Jesus Christ. (1 Peter 1:2 NLT)

For this reason I kneel before the Father . . . I pray that out of his glorious riches he may strengthen you with power through his Spirit in your inner being, so that Christ may dwell in your hearts through faith. And I pray that you, being rooted and established in love, may have power, together with all the Lord's holy people, to grasp how wide and long and high and deep is the love of Christ, and to know this love that surpasses knowledge—that you may be filled to the measure of all the fullness of God. (Ephesians 3:14–19)

How much more, then, will the blood of Christ, who through the eternal Spirit offered himself unblemished to God, cleanse our consciences from acts that lead to death, so that we may serve the living God! (Hebrews 9:14)

Do not get drunk on wine, which leads to debauchery. Instead, be filled with the Spirit, speaking to one another with psalms, hymns, and songs from the Spirit. Sing and make music from your heart to the Lord, always giving thanks to God the Father for everything, in the name of our Lord Jesus Christ. (Ephesians 5:18–20)

Keep watch over yourselves and all the flock of which the Holy Spirit has made you overseers. Be shepherds of the church of God, which he bought with his own blood. (Acts 20:28)

GOD'S REVELATION OF HIMSELF

I noticed that Jesus made no serious attempt to explain the tri-unity of God or to prove it to the people to whom He was speaking.

217

We read in the Gospel that Jesus said, "My teaching is not my own. It comes from the one who sent me. Anyone who chooses to do the will of God will find out whether my teaching comes from God or whether I speak on my own" (John 7:16–17).

My dear reader, God reveals the Trinity to those who desire to know Him and do His will. This is something that God does not easily allow to be projected to the world and trampled on. Through understanding the Trinity, God is inviting sinners into an intimate relationship with Him, to experience Him as Father, and to be united to Him forever based on His grace and mercy. We read in the Bible: "For through him [Jesus] we both have access to the Father by one Spirit [Holy Spirit]" (Ephesians 2:18).

One day Jesus was alone with His disciples and asked them a question: "Who do people say the Son of Man is?" (Matthew 16:13) They replied, people are not sure who You are, but they agree that You are a prophet (v. 14). Then, Jesus asked them,

"But what about you? Who do you say I am?"

Simon Peter answered, "You are the Messiah, the Son of the Living God."

Jesus replied, "Blessed are you, Simon son of Jonah, for this was not revealed to you by flesh and blood, but by my Father in heaven." (Matthew 16:15–17)

Note, Jesus did not tell Peter that he was smarter than the others, but that he was blessed because his insight came only from God.

Any revelation of God's truth is a manifestation of His grace. The tri-unity of God is the highest revelation God makes of Himself to His people as they sincerely and wholeheartedly seek Him.

My dear reader, I will do my best in this book to help you understand. But without a special revelation from God to your heart, mind, and soul, you will never believe.

The Bible teaches that the nature of God is compound, which means there is plurality in the oneness of God. In the book of Genesis we read: "Then God said, 'Let *us* make man in *our* image, in *our* likeness, so that they may rule over the fish in the sea and the birds in the sky, over the livestock and all the wild animals, and over all the creatures that move along the ground.' So God created mankind in *his* own image, in the image of God *he* created him; male and female *he* created them" (Genesis 1:26–27, italics added). The italics added in these verses emphasize the combination of singular and plural pronouns revealing the compound unity of God.

The Bible confirms the following truths:

1. God is one. He is also unique and undivided.
2. Within this one being there are three divine persons.
3. These divine persons are the Father, the Son, and the Holy Spirit.
4. The relationship among these divine persons is eternal. They have eternally existed within the being of God.

Note that when we refer to three persons in the one triune God, this word "person" is used in a different sense from its normal use in relation to human beings. Again, God is infinite. Of course, the word "persons" is not adequate to express the divine concept. We must get out of our minds any human analogy. However, each possesses intelligence, emotion, and will.

Note that all true Christians believe in one God (Tawhid), and they regard *polytheists* (those who believe in more than one God) as unbelievers. God is one. This oneness of God is the most essential characteristic of the Trinity. The unity of God allows for the existence of three personal distinctions in the divine nature.

MISUNDERSTANDING OF
THE CHRISTIAN DOCTRINE OF THE TRINITY

Many Muslims mistakenly think that Christians believe in three gods: Mary, Jesus, and God. On this issue, Ibn Abbas writes: "What is meant by the Trinity is God the most high, His consort, and His Son."[1]

I will briefly mention some of the reasons behind this misunderstanding:

The Arabic Word *Thalatha* Is Mistranslated as "Trinity"

Thalatha appears nineteen times in the Qur'an where it is correctly translated as "three." Unfortunately, the word *thalatha* was mistranslated as "Trinity" by Abdullah Yusuf Ali. His translation of Surah 4:171 (from Arabic to English) reads, "Say not 'Trinity'" (The Qur'an in Arabic states "say not thalatha"). Again, thalatha only means "three," and it is certainly different from the word "Trinity," which means three in the unity of one (Pickthall's translation to this verse is accurate).

Also, in Yusuf Ali's translation of the Arabic Qur'an (Surah 5:73), he mistranslated the simple Arabic words *Thaalithu thalatha*. He made them mean "one of three in a Trinity," instead of the obvious and only meaning "the third one of three."

Consider the problem that the majority of the Muslim world has by not understanding the Arabic language of the Qur'an. When they read this verse in English, they automatically assume that the Qur'an rejects the biblical belief in the triune God (Trinity). Abdullah Yusuf Ali's translation is widely distributed all over the world.

The Arabic Qur'an Contains No Reference to the Christian Doctrine of the Triune God

Neither the correctly translated *word* Trinity nor the Christian *concept* of the Trinity appear at all in the original Arabic Qur'anic text. The Qur'an never mentions that Christians believe in God as Father, Son, and Holy Spirit.

The Qur'an Just Rejects the Belief in Three Separate Gods

The Qur'an misrepresents the Trinity as a family of Allah, Mary, and Jesus. For example, Surah 5:73 states: "They do blaspheme who say: Allah is one of three in a Trinity." The Qur'an named these three gods as Jesus, His mother Mary, and Allah as we read in Surah 5:116, which states: "O Jesus the son of Mary! Didst thou say unto men, 'Worship me and my mother as gods in derogation of Allah'?"

We read in Surah 5:75: "Christ, the son of Mary, was no more than a Messenger. . . . His mother was a woman of truth. They had both to eat their (daily) food." The Qur'an explains that Jesus and Mary couldn't be gods because they needed to eat food to survive. So, like everybody else, they were both humans, because God does not need any sustenance.

The famous Muslim commentator Zamakhashari commented on the word *thalatha* in Surah 4:171: "According to the evidence of the Qur'an, the Christian maintains that God, Christ, and Mary are three gods."

Although the Qur'an denounces the doctrine of the existence of three gods, this should not be confused with the Christian doctrine of the Holy Trinity. The Holy Trinity is one God, and within this divine unity there are three eternal Persons of one substance and power.

There is no evidence that Christians ever actually believed that the Trinity consisted of God, Jesus, and Mary.

Unfortunately, the excessive prayers given to Mary by some misguided Christian sects, which are contrary to the teaching of the Bible, led Muhammad to misconceive the true meaning of the Trinity. Muhammad mistakenly thought that some Christians believe and teach that the Virgin Mary is one of the persons of the triune God. Muhammad did not have adequate information for correct understanding of the doctrine of the Trinity.

Apparently, Muhammad was unable to recognize the vast difference between the Christian belief in Jesus as the unique eternal Son of God and the pagan Arab belief in their goddesses as daughters of God. He assumed both beliefs to be identical in character.

We read in the Qur'an: "The Jews call Uzayr a son of God, and the Christians call Christ the Son of God. . . . (In this) they but imitate what the Unbelievers of old used to say" (Surah 9:30).

It seems that Muhammad was completely unaware that the God of the Bible, whom all true Christians worship, is Father, Son, and Holy Spirit in one eternal, divine being.

The Qur'an misrepresents the biblical and historic Christian position on the Trinity and only presents Muhammad's limited knowledge and misconception of it. My precious Muslim reader, please allow me to ask a sincere and serious question: The Qur'an was written hundreds of years after the spread of the Bible in so many parts of the world, so why don't we find in the pages of the Qur'an any words that even remotely represent the true Christian doctrine of the tri-unity of God?

Regarding the Qur'anic verse: "They do blaspheme who say: Allah is one of three" (Surah 5:73), Christians agree with this statement because we believe that God is one and only one. He cannot be one of three.

The Qur'an also states: "They do blaspheme who say: Allah is Christ the son of Mary" (Surah 5:72). We agree with this verse because it is not stated anywhere in the Bible that God is Christ the son of Mary. The Bible states instead, "That God was reconciling the world to himself in Christ" (2 Corinthians 5:19). There were heresies in the early Christian centuries that taught that Christ was God the Father. Although the Word of God reveals that Christ is God because of His divine nature, the Bible never confined God to the person of the Son (Christ) alone.

The Qur'an Teaches That Christians Are Monotheistic

On the other hand, the Qur'an actually testifies that Christians ("people of the Book") are monotheistic (they worship one God) and they are not infidels (idolaters). The following passage from Surah 29:46 is an example:

> And dispute ye not with the people of the Book, except with means better (than mere disputation) . . . but say, "We believe in the Revelation which has come down to us and in that which came down to you; our God and your God is One; and it is to Him we bow (in Islam)."

This verse affirms that Christians worship the true God. (Read also Surah 2:139.)

Surah 2:62 and Surah 3:113–114 also confirm that the revelation that the Jews and Christians received was from the only true and living God.

Note that Arab Christians called God "Allah" centuries before the time of Muhammad. Today, Arab Christians all over the world still call God "Allah." The word "Allah" is not found only in the Qur'an, but also in all Arabic Bibles. Incidentally, the Arabic word for God is *Ilah*, which is similar to the word for

God in other Semitic languages (Aramaic: *Elah*; Syriac: *Alaha*; Hebrew: *El, Elohim*).

So *Ilah* is the Arabic word for God. *Allah* is this same word combined with the definite article, meaning "the God," which means "the One and only God."

I am sure that you know that Islam forbids the Muslim man to marry an idolatress, but it does not forbid him to marry a Christian, because Christians are people who know the one God and worship only Him.

It is important to mention here that although the Roman Catholic, Orthodox, and Protestant branches disagree on some doctrines, they have never disagreed about the doctrine of the Trinity, not even in its slightest details. The reason is because the entire Bible clearly teaches this fundamental Christian belief in the triune nature of God.

26

UNDERSTANDING THE TRI-UNITY (TRINITY) OF GOD

The knowledge of the triune God is something that has to be spiritually discerned.

There isn't any symbol in the physical universe that can adequately describe the tri-unity of God as taught in the Bible. However, the symbol that appears above is made of one continuous line, attempting to convey the one eternal Godhead with three distinct Persons. All three—the Father, Son, and Holy Spirit—are distinct yet interconnected.

THE TRIUNE GOD IS UNIMAGINABLE

The impossibility of imagining the tri-unity of God indicates that humans did not invent this doctrine. It is not surprising that it is impossible for us to imagine the God who created and controls the world. The fullness of God's nature lies outside our experience and knowledge.

God is a Person, different from any human person, because He is a Spirit. His Spirit fills the whole universe. God decided to speak to us and come to our earth in the person of Jesus Christ, who is the Word of God. God also decided to dwell through the Person of His Holy Spirit in every person who believes in Jesus Christ.

THERE IS COMPLEXITY WITHIN UNITY

God's oneness is not merely a simple, single unit as a table or a chair. Consider that each human is one, but his unity is more complex than that of a one-celled bacteria. The oneness of man involves spiritual aspects as well as physical. Because God is Spirit, infinite, and eternal, His being is beyond our imagination.

Trinity Means Three in the Unity of One

Father, Son, and Holy Spirit are one in essence, will, and nature. Christians believe in one God, eternally existing as Father, Son, and Holy Spirit.

Many of my Muslim friends think that this doctrine of the Trinity contradicts itself. They ask, "How can something be three and one at the same time?" In response, biblical scholar Dean Halverson explains:

For a statement to contradict itself it must both affirm and deny the same thing in the same respect. Does the doctrine of the Trinity do that? The answer is no, because the doctrine states that God is one essence (or being) and three in person. Essence and personhood are different. God is three in person, in that each person of the Trinity is distinct within the Godhead. God is one, in that each person of the Godhead shares the same self-existing essence and other qualities unique to God. This simultaneous distinction and sameness is seen in John 1:1.[1]

Each Person in the Trinity Is Called "God"

While each of the three Persons within the one God performs specific functions (more than the other two Persons), nonetheless all three are continuously involved in everything together. The Father, Son, and Holy Spirit are bound together in such a close unity that the life of each flows through each of the others.

Clearly the Bible teaches that each of the three distinct Persons is called *God*. First, the Holy Spirit is called God. For example, in Acts 5:3–4 we see that the Holy Spirit is identified as God and also is seen as a distinct Person. (See also Acts 13:2; John 3:5–6; Romans 8:9; 1 Corinthians 2:10–11; 2 Corinthians 3:17–18.)

The Father is repeatedly called God (1 Peter 1:2; Galatians 1:1; Ephesians 1:3; and 1 Corinthians 8:6).

Jesus is called God as well (Romans 9:5; Titus 2:13; Acts 20:28; Matthew 1:21–23). Considering all the revealed biblical teachings on the nature of God, the clear conclusion is that there are three Persons in the one Godhead.

Each one of us is one finitely. God is one infinitely. Within the infinite realm of God there are three distinct personalities, and they are named the Father, the Son, and the Holy Spirit.

HELPFUL MUSLIM EXPLANATIONS

Al-Ghazzali answered a similar question about tri-unity. He is one of the most respected Muslim theologians in the history of Islam. He wrote:

How can the many be one? Know that this is the goal of all revelations, and the secrets of this science should not be penned down in a book, for the people of knowledge said, the unveiling of the secret of Lordship is blasphemy. . . . The thing can be many in one sense, but also can be one in another sense. And so, as man is many in one sense if you look at his spirit and body and limbs and blood vessels and bones and members, but in another sense, he is one man.[2]

Even the famous Muslim Imam Shaarani acknowledges: "Conventional plurality does not preclude essential unity, such as the branches of a tree in relation to its root or the fingers in relation to the palm."[3]

THREE CAN BE IN ONE

Through an experiment known as the triple point of water, it is possible for water (one substance) to exist simultaneously as ice (solid), steam (gas), and water (liquid). The sun consists of material, light, and heat.

Heat and light will come out of the flame of the fire; wherever there is a flame, light and heat exist. The flame, the light, and the heat are three manifestations of one fire, they are not three fires.

The Nature of God's Oneness

Although the word "Trinity" is not in the Bible, the concept is clearly biblical. Also, the word *tawhid*, which Muslims usually use to describe God, is not in the Qur'an.

Christians agree with Muslims that God is one—entirely distinct from all created beings. But we have not yet begun to deal with the issue of what mysteries the divine nature may contain within itself. Mysteries are inherent in the supreme divine nature of God. Therefore, whatever our beliefs, whether we hold on to the Muslim belief about the *singular oneness* of God's nature or the Christian belief in the *compound unity* of God's nature, neither conflicts with oneness. We are dealing simply with the *inner* nature of that essence. Muslims are taught that God's nature is a single unity. The Bible teaches us that it is a complex unity.

Christianity, Judaism, and Islam are all monotheistic. They firmly and equally teach that God is one. The conflict deals with understanding and defining God's divine unity. Again, God's nature surpasses the capacity of our minds to fully imagine. To argue that the Christian belief in God is against reason is simply to make oneself the judge of what God can or cannot be, which is blasphemy. After all, God is the Potter and we are merely the clay!

God's Nature Cannot Be Fully Expressed

The non-Christian reader must agree that in using words such as "Father," "Son," and "Holy Spirit," God is using human terms for our benefit. It is God through His grace accommodating Himself to human limitations and ignorance, just as, for example, a human father must use simple language when trying to explain something very complex to a child.

So there is no human language suitable to express the realities of the divine nature. The relationship between the Persons of the Godhead transcends all human thought and language.

Many Muslims state that they cannot believe in the doctrine of the Trinity, because in their minds, it has not been proven. However, again, the problem is not in the doctrine itself but in the limitations of the human mind.

Even though we are able, for the most part, to accurately describe everything that we can see, the truth is we cannot use finite human standards to define the unseen, infinite Creator.

It is wrong to conclude that because three persons on earth cannot be absolutely one in essence and nature, therefore Father, Son, and Holy Spirit cannot be one. We must acknowledge that because God is infinite, Spirit, and eternal, His unity must be of a character different from that which we see, expect, or imagine.

A doctrine of God that can be imagined in the human mind most likely was invented by the human mind in the first place. The very fact that no human can imagine the tri-unity of God is not evidence to the weakness of the Christian doctrine. Rather, it is evidence that it is true because the essence of the true God is beyond human imagination.

Biblical scholar Kenneth Cragg has said, "A doctrine of God does not commend itself by its ability to be reduced to a statement on a postage stamp."

The doctrine of the Trinity is not contrary to reason; it is above the realms of finite human reasoning.

God desires for us to love Him and obey Him. He did not create us to analyze Him. It is wrong for anyone to try to put God in a laboratory in order to examine Him. It is also impossible to try to reduce God to fit a formula.

Spiritual Revelations Are Considered Truth Even When Not Provable

Let me pose a question: If an atheist asked for proof for the many beliefs Muslims hold as truths, would it be possible for you as a Muslim to prove them? For example, consider the Muslim belief in the resurrection of the dead. If an atheist asked you how it would be possible for the dead to be raised back to life, could you satisfactorily explain and prove it? It is not possible to do so through human logic or intellect alone.

My point is that if you allow yourself to reject the tri-unity of God because Christians cannot absolutely prove it with intellectual arguments, then you cannot blame the atheist for rejecting the belief in God's revelation that cannot be proven. Mankind must accept by faith what God has revealed in the Bible about His nature.

Note that according to the Qur'an and the Hadith, Allah has a face, hands, fingers, feet, and eyes (Surah 55:27 and Surah 38:75). The highly influential Muslim scholar and jurist Imam Abu Hanifah teaches: "The most high has a hand and face and soul without asking how."[4]

My dear Muslim reader, do you believe that Jesus performed miracles? I am sure that your answer is yes. You believe that Jesus performed miracles even though you never saw Him perform one, but you believe because the Qur'an stated that Jesus performed the greatest miracles.

We followers of Christ also submit and believe in the triune God because that is what the Bible revealed God to be.

Human logic and reason alone are insufficient to lead to the full knowledge of God's nature. As we read in the Bible, "Can you fathom the mysteries of God? Can you probe the limits of the Almighty? They are higher than the heavens—what can you do? They are deeper than the depths below—what can you know?" (Job 11:7–8).

THE MYSTERY OF THE TRINITY

I know of a devout follower of Jesus Christ who was thinking hard trying to understand everything about the tri-unity of God. He became very frustrated, even angry at times, because he was not able to figure out everything about the tri-unity of God.

One day, he was walking on the beach and again thinking hard about the Trinity. He saw a child running back and forth trying to carry in his hands water from the ocean and put it in a hole in the sand. God guided the man's thoughts through what he saw. He realized the futility of his attempts to contain the complexity of God in his mind, as it is impossible for the child to bring the ocean into a small hole by his hands.

FUNCTIONS OF THE PERSONS WITHIN THE TRINITY

The purpose of God's revelation to us in the Gospel is:

- To guide us to know Him as our heavenly Father,
- To experience His forgiveness through Jesus Christ, and
- To enjoy His divine presence through the Holy Spirit.

God wants us to have the right relationship with Him in order to worship, love, obey Him, and know that we are going to heaven. And that should be good enough for all of us. Biblical scholar G. Parrinder explains:

God as . . . provider is seen in the Father who cares for mankind. The essential nature of God as love manifesting Himself in action is seen in the "Son," . . . [while on earth] his loving actions and words, his suffering and death. The ever-present nature of God is seen in the [Holy] Spirit. Yet these three are one, the threefold revelation of God to men.[5]

YOU CAN KNOW GOD'S LOVE, POWER, AND SALVATION EXPERIENTIALLY

It grieves my heart that Muslim theologians, based only on the Qur'an, and ignoring biblical revelation, teach that God's nature is merely simple and singular. This leaves people with an empty and incomplete concept of God. By rigidly insisting on simplicity in God's nature, they tragically and unknowingly deprive their followers of experiencing the salvation, love, and power of God personally. They make God distant, so unreachable and inaccessible.

Muslim teachers teach that the Allah of Islam has simple, strict unity that can be easily understood by the human mind, yet they confirm that Allah cannot be personally known.

The amazing truth is the triune God the Bible reveals to us is a knowable God. He can be known and experienced right within the depth of the human heart (as you will fully discover after reading chapters 29 and 30).

God's Nature Is Love

It is significant to notice that because God is a loving God and His nature is unchangeable, His attribute of love must have existed from all eternity. Since love must have an object, the question arises: Before God created any living being, whom did He love? The answer is clear: Within the divine unity, there must have existed at least a lover and a beloved. The Bible reveals that there always have been three Persons within God enjoying love—mutually exercised, expressed, and experienced.

According to the Bible, God is love. Love can never be exercised in isolation. God cannot be love and also solitary.

Only the Christian doctrine of the triune God explains how the attribute of love exists in God's divine nature. The God of the Gospel is not singular and totally alone. He is the all-sufficient God who is able to exist by Himself in love. God wasn't lonely before He created humans. The Father, Son, and Holy Spirit existed in a state of complete, fulfilling fellowship.

It is important here to mention that God created us not because He was all alone and He needed to receive worship or anything from us.

The truth is, God, as described in the Bible, created you and desires to have a relationship with you, so you can glorify Him (1 Peter 4:11) and enjoy Him forever (1 Thess. 4:17). He wants you and me to enjoy what He has, because He loves us.

Difference in Function Does Not Indicate Inferiority of Nature

Long before humans existed, the Father, the Son, and the Holy Spirit chose the roles they would take in the plan for the salvation of the human race.

The one who took the function of the source of all things, including creation, is called the Father; the one who came to earth as our Savior is called the Son; and the one who indwells believers is called the Holy Spirit. The Son and the Holy Spirit are subject to the Father.

Muslim teachers mistakenly assume that Jesus Christ can't be God because He lived on earth as a man. Their wrong assumption is because Jesus' function gave Him an inferior status to the Father's; therefore, He must have been inferior in nature.

We cannot ignore this commonsense truth: nature and function are two different things. To illustrate, depending on the season of life, one spouse's function may be doing more household duties and taking care of the children, etc., but this does not make them less human or inferior to the other spouse, who sits in a nice office spending the day looking at papers and talking on the phone.

Even though Jesus told us that He and the Father have the same nature (John 10:30), He also said to His disciples, "If you loved me, you would be glad that I am going to the Father, for the Father is greater than I" (John 14:28). Jesus is not speaking in this verse about His nature but is rather speaking of His lowly position while living on earth.

Jesus meant that the Father is greater in office and glory than Jesus was in His humiliated status on earth.

God the Father never came into the world as man to be cruelly treated; but Jesus, while living on earth, was despised by many. From this perspective, Jesus meant that God the Father is greater in His position. While on earth, Jesus' function was subordinate and submissive to the Father.

Jesus was telling His disciples to rejoice because He will be returning to the place He had with the Father before the world was (John 17:5). He would no longer be the subject of attack and ridicule by the Jewish religious leaders. Instead, He would be at the right hand of the Father in heaven itself.

The term "greater" speaks of the position of the Father in heaven over the position of the Son on earth. The Son would soon be leaving this humbled position and returning to His position of glory.

Capturing Glimpses of the Trinity

Noted church historian Philip Schaff summarizes the biblical concept of the Trinity:

God is one in three persons [that is, three distinct persons of the same nature]. . . . The divine persons are in one another and form a perpetual intercommunication and motion within the divine essence. Each person has all the divine attributes which are inherent in the divine essence but each has also a characteristic individuality . . . which is peculiar to the person . . . but the three persons are co-eternal and co-equal.[6]

Finally, my dear reader, when you put your faith in Jesus Christ, God Himself will make you understand with certainty that He is the Father who loves you, and He is Jesus Christ who gave Himself for you, and He is the Holy Spirit who indwells you.

If you ask me "How will I know?" I will share with you a story that I read of a young boy who was outside flying a kite. The kite went so high (up and up) that it was hidden by the clouds. A man asked the young boy, "What are you doing?"

The boy replied, "I am flying a kite."

The man asked, "Are you sure? I can't see anything."

The boy replied, "I know it is up there because every little while I feel a tug."

My Muslim reader, only when you put your faith in Jesus Christ will you experience the triune nature of God.

27

JESUS IS THE ETERNAL SON OF GOD IN A UNIQUE SPIRITUAL SENSE

The expression "Son of God" confirms that Jesus was not the son of any man, but that He came directly from God.

THE QUR'AN'S VIEW OF JESUS' SONSHIP

Based on many passages in the Qur'an, such as Surah 2:116, Surah 6:101, Surah 9:30, Surah 18:4, and Surah 19:35, many Muslims misunderstand the Christian belief in the Fatherhood of God and Sonship of Jesus, incorrectly assuming that God had to have a consort (partner in a sexual relation). In Surah 6:101, the question is asked, "How can He have a son when He hath no consort?"

It seems that Muhammad only understood the title Son of God in finite and human terms. Another verse in the Qur'an states, "And exalted is the Majesty of our Lord: He has taken neither a wife nor a son" (Surah 72:3).

What the Qur'an rejects as untrue is the carnal idea that God had a son through a physical relationship with a partner. Such an idea is blasphemous also to Christians, who reject such a notion.

THE BIBLE'S VIEW OF JESUS' SONSHIP

When the Gospel states that Christ is the divine Son of God, it does not mean that Christ came by procreation. His Sonship was not the result of a physical relationship between a father and mother. It is of another kind—an eternal, spiritual Sonship, this Father-Son relationship has existed from eternity. Please remember that we believe that Jesus, the eternal Son of God, is united in one Spirit with God the Father from all eternity. The Son took on an additional human nature and dwelt among us. He came to this earth as God's ambassador and was subject to God's authority.

Jesus' Sonship Is Not a Physical (Earthly) Relationship

When the Gospel teaches that Jesus is "the Son of God," it means God was revealed in His essential nature of love in Christ. Biblical scholar Kenneth Cragg presents an analogy: "When we speak of Beethoven the musician, or Leonardo da Vinci the artist, we mean these men and their full personality in a particular capacity. Capacities which do not preclude their having others, but yet involving them wholly."[1]

In physical birth there is a separation between mother and child. But Jesus came from the Father without leaving Him. Jesus appeared in human form and yet remained in God. Jesus said, "I am in the Father, and . . . the Father is in me" (John 14:10).

God's Only Begotten Son

When I refer to Jesus as the Son of God, many Muslims recite Surah 112, "He begetteth not, nor begotten." Yes, God was never born because He is eternal. And, yes, it is true that God does not beget according to the Qur'an's use of the word "beget"—in which one becomes a father by sexual means to "beget" a son—for He is Spirit, not human. In order for God to be called "Father," He does not need to beget in the way we humans do. Mary conceived by the Holy Spirit—not by human flesh—which is the glad tidings of the one-time, holy, pure conception!

Surah 3:46–47 documented Mary's conversation with the angel: "How can I have a child when no man hath touched me?"

The Gospel also documented the conversation in Luke 1:34–35: "'How will this be,' Mary asked the angel, 'since I am a virgin?' The angel answered, 'The Holy Spirit will come on you, and the power of the Most High will overshadow you. So the holy one to be born will be called the Son of God.'"

Certain English translations of the Gospel state, "For God so loved the world that he gave his one and only Son, that whoever believes in him shall not perish but have eternal life" (John 3:16). Some other Bible translations read that God gave His "only begotten Son." The Greek word that is translated as "begotten" in the original text is *monogenae*, which means "the one" (mono) and "coming from" (genae) or "the one coming from." In other words, Jesus came from the Father. The expression "only begotten" or monogenes does not refer to physical begetting but to uniqueness, "one of a kind."

Some translators of the Bible translated this word as "only" while others use "only begotten." Both are correct because the meaning is the same—the only divine Son coming directly from God the Father.

The Gospel teaches us that Christ is eternal. He existed before Abraham. Jesus told some Jewish people: "Before Abraham was born, I am!" (John 8:58). He was before the world came into being (John 17:5, 24).

Who Else Could Jesus' Father Be?

Both the Bible and the Qur'an teach as a fact that Jesus was born of a virgin, conceived through God's Spirit. We read in the Qur'an that Jesus is called "a Spirit from God." According to the Gospel and the Qur'an, Jesus is not related to any human father. Therefore, He is related to God, the heavenly Father. If you object to Jesus being called the "Son of God" in the Bible, can you then explain who else Jesus' Father could be?

To reason that God cannot have a son without a wife is to assume God has our human limitations. It would be the same as reasoning that God cannot have life without breathing. Although it is true that anything that lives must breathe, God of course does not depend on breathing to live and yet He lives. The Gospel explains that "God is spirit" (John 4:24) and Almighty.

The Arabic word *walad* means "a son born of sexual relations." And certainly Jesus is not a son in this sense. However, there is another Arabic word for son: *ibn*, which can be used without indicating sexual union. For example, because I was born and raised in Egypt, you can call me "the son of the Nile" or "the son of Egypt."

No one has the right to forbid anything to God (such as having a Son), which He does not forbid Himself. God is greater than all. No one has the liberty to set limitations on God, because God is able to do anything and is sovereign (Supreme in Authority)!

JESUS' RELATIONAL FUNCTION

The very title *"Son of God"* immediately suggests Jesus' relational function. Consider that an earthly father and his son share the same human nature, yet the son is subject to his father. Likewise, the expression "Son of God" indicates relationship between the first two persons of the triune God. God the Father and Jesus share the same divine nature, yet Jesus subjected *Himself* to the authority of the Father. Therefore, we see that the expression Son of God indicates likeness or sameness of nature.

The Son took human form more than two thousand years ago and became the man Jesus Christ. Jesus came to earth to do His Father's will and to glorify His heavenly Father.

The title "Son of God" is the best language possible to express the close and unique relationship that Jesus Christ has with God the Father. The Bible reveals to us about Jesus: "For in Christ all the fullness of the Deity lives in bodily form" (Colossians 2:9). Jesus is the visible expression of the invisible God. We rejoice that Jesus came to earth to reveal God to us, and that God did not remain entirely hidden in His glorious majesty far from His creation! As stated in Hebrews 1:1–3, "In the past God spoke to our ancestors through the prophets at many times and in various ways, but in these last days he has spoken to us by his Son. . . . The Son is the radiance of God's glory and the exact representation of his being."

Jesus Teaches That He Is the Son of God

After Jesus healed a man born blind, we read in the Gospel that Jesus asked him: "'Do you believe in the Son of God?' He answered and said, 'Who is He, Lord, that I may believe in Him?' And Jesus said to him, 'You have both seen Him and it is He who is talking with you'" (John 9:35–38 NKJV).

Jesus referred to Himself as the Son of God in absolute and exclusive terms. We read in the Bible that Jesus said, "No one knows the Son except the Father, and no one knows the Father except the Son" (Matthew 11:27). Jesus said, "Anyone who loves me will obey my teaching. My Father will love them, and we will come to them and make our home with them" (John 14:23).

If Jesus were nothing more than a human being He would have been committing blasphemy when He said "that all may honor the Son just as they honor the Father. Whoever does not honor the Son does not honor the Father, who sent him" (John 5:23).

Jesus also said, "Anyone who has seen me has seen the Father. . . . Don't you believe that I am in the Father, and that the Father is in me? . . . Believe me . . . or at least believe on the evidence of the works themselves" (John 14:9–11).

Let us look at one example that demonstrates Jesus' claim to be the unique Son of God: The Parable of the Tenants and the Vineyard. In Luke chapter 20, Jesus teaches a crowd of people about God the Father and Himself:

> A man planted a vineyard, rented it to some farmers and went away for a long time. At harvest time he sent a servant to the tenants so they would give him some of the fruit of the vineyard. But the tenants beat him and sent him away empty-handed. He sent another servant, but that one also they beat and treated shamefully and sent away empty-handed. He sent still a third, and they wounded him and threw him out. Then the owner of the vineyard said, "What shall I do? I will send my son, whom I love; perhaps they will respect him." But when the tenants saw him, they talked the matter over. "This is the heir," they said. "Let's kill him, and the inheritance will be ours." So they threw him out of the vineyard and killed him. What then will the owner of the vineyard do to them? He will come and kill those tenants and give the vineyard to others. When the people [the religious leaders at the time] heard this, they said, "God forbid!" (Luke 20:9–16; see also Matthew 21:33–43)

Interpretation of the Biblical Parable

The characters in this parable of the tenants and the vineyard are identified as follows:

- The owner of the vineyard is God the Father, who planted the vineyard.
- The landowner's son is Jesus Christ, the Messiah.
- The vineyard is the nation of Israel.
- The tenants are the Jewish religious leaders at that time.
- The landowner's servants are the prophets sent to the nation of Israel.

Jesus' Message in This Parable

In this parable, Jesus presented Himself as the son sent from the owner of the vineyard. Those tenant farmers in charge of tending the vineyard killed the owner's son. The Jewish leaders understood what Jesus was saying—that He was applying this story directly to them and pointing at them as the tenant farmers in His story. We read, "The teachers of the law and the chief priests looked for a way to arrest him immediately, because they knew he had spoken this parable against them. But they were afraid of the people" (Luke 20:19).

Clearly, Jesus' parable teaches that God the Father sent many prophets to the people of Israel to ask them to produce the "good fruits" of righteousness. But the Jewish leadership rejected the prophets and mistreated them. Then God the Father sent His only beloved Son. However, the Jewish people rejected Him as well and killed Him. Jesus went to the vineyard in submission to His Father's will.

Jesus Confronted the Jewish Religious Leaders

In the Gospel account by the apostle John, Jesus Himself defends His claim to be the divine Son of God. He declares:

"What about the one whom the Father set apart as his very own and sent into the world? Why then do you accuse me of blasphemy because I said, 'I am God's Son'? Do not believe me unless I do the works of my Father. But if I do them, even though you do not believe me, believe the works, that you may know and understand that the Father is in me, and I in the Father." Again they [the religious leaders at the time] tried to seize him. (John 10:36–39)

The Gospel of John recorded that after Jesus healed a sick man on the Sabbath day, the Jews were persecuting Him. Jesus said to them, "'My Father is always at his work to this very day, and I too am working.' For this reason they tried all the more to kill him; not only was he breaking the Sabbath, but he was even calling God his own Father, making himself equal with God" (John 5:17–18).

Jesus did not tell them their interpretation of His words was wrong. Instead He offered more teaching to confirm His identity. (Please read John 5:19–26.)

On another occasion, the high priest asked Jesus, "'Are you the Messiah, the Son of the Blessed One?' 'I am,' said Jesus" (Mark 14:61–62). This is an absolute declaration.

Ultimately, Jesus' claim to be the Son of God is what caused the unbelieving Jews to consider Him worthy of death (Matthew 26:63–65; Mark 14:61–63; Luke 22:70).

We read in the Bible that when Pilate told the Jewish leaders, "I find no basis for a charge against him," they replied, "We have a law, and according to that law he must die, because he claimed to be the Son of God" (John 19:6–7).

John writes,

> For God so loved the world that he gave his one and only Son, that whoever believes in him shall not perish but have eternal life. For God did not send his Son into the world to condemn the world, but to save the world through him. Whoever believes in him is not condemned, but whoever does not believe stands condemned already because they have not believed in the name of God's one and only Son. (John 3:16–18)

Jesus prayed, "And now, Father, glorify me in your presence with the glory I had with you before the world began" (John 17:5).

Jesus taught that God is His Father and that He is the Son of God. We respond by believing in faith in what God has revealed about Himself. Human reason should not be the final judge.

We Believe in the Word of God

The Bible teaches: "But when the set time had fully come, God sent his Son, born of a woman" (Galatians 4:4). The Lord Jesus is the only begotten Son, who was born from (came from) the essence of the Father before all ages. Therefore, He who was born of the Virgin Mary was the Son of God and at the same time the Son of Man as Jesus called Himself.

We read in Luke "God sent the angel Gabriel . . . to a virgin" named Mary (vv. 1:26–27). The angel told her: "You will conceive and give birth to a son, and you are to call him Jesus. He will . . . be called the Son of the Most High" (vv. 31–32).

"How will this be," Mary asked the angel, "since I am a virgin?" The angel answered, "The Holy Spirit will come on you, and the power of the Most High will overshadow you. So the holy one to be born will be called the Son of God. . . . For no word from God will ever fail" (vv. 34–35, 37).

By the action of the Holy Spirit in the womb of the Virgin Mary, the divine nature was united with the human nature, which Jesus received from the Virgin Mary. God Himself descended and was incarnated.

The Holy Spirit purified the Virgin's womb. The flesh formed in her body was the only begotten Son.

Man cannot be the final judge on the truth of who God is and who Jesus is. Man should only submit to what God has revealed. You cannot rely on the dim light of human reasoning to judge the infinite, eternal, and most glorious being.

It is significant that not only did Jesus Himself claim to be the Son of God, but John the Baptist and God the Father also testified to this eternal truth. John the Baptist declared, "I have seen and testified that this is the Son of God" (John 1:34 NKJV).

We also read in the Bible the testimony of God the Father when John the Baptist was baptizing Jesus: "As soon as Jesus was baptized, he went up out of the water. At that moment heaven was opened, and he saw the Spirit of God descending like a dove and alighting on him. And a voice from heaven said, 'This is my Son, whom I love; with him I am well pleased'" (Matthew 3:16–17).

The Holy Spirit inspired the writing of the apostle John, who was one of Jesus' disciples and an eyewitness to Jesus' life, death, resurrection, and ascension. We read: "For there are three that bear witness in heaven: the Father, the Word, and the Holy Spirit; and these three are one" (1 John 5:7 NKJV).

The witness of the Holy Spirit about Jesus was also evident through the testimony of the prophets, including John the Baptist.

God continues to speak to us in the same chapter: "If we receive the witness of men, the witness of God is greater: for this is the witness of God which He has testified of His Son. He who believes in the Son of God has the witness in himself" (verses 9–10a NKJV).

Those words mean when you believe in God's testimony about Jesus, God will put the truth in your heart. You will know the truth in your inner being. You will have within you an actual verification of God's own faithful words.

The passage from above continues:

> He who does not believe God has made Him a liar, because he has not believed the testimony that God has given of His Son. And this is the testimony: that God has given us eternal life, and this life is in His Son. He who has the Son has life; he who does not have the Son of God does not have life. (1 John 5:10b–12 NKJV)

Jesus said: "He who believes in Me, believes not in Me, but in Him who sent Me. . . . I have not spoken on My own authority; but the Father who sent Me gave Me a command, what I should say and what I should speak" (John 12:44, 49 NKJV).

God, the King of kings, sent His Son (the Prince) to all people. The Son looks like His Father, carries the seal of the kingdom, delivers the words of the King, and accomplishes the will of the King. If anyone rejects the Son, he automatically rejects the King.

SECTION TEN

WORSHIP, LOVE, AND THE SAVIOR

28

JESUS RECEIVED WORSHIP

t is significant that early Muslim theologians agreed with the teaching of the Gospel that Jesus is worthy to receive worship.

JESUS IS WORTHY TO RECEIVE WORSHIP

Early Islamic scholar Ibn Ishaq[1] quotes a letter sent by Muhammad to the Negus of Abyssinia. In it Muhammad said, "I bear witness that Jesus, son of Mary, is the Spirit of God and His Word, which he cast to Mary the virgin."[2]

According to the teaching of early reputable Muslim scholars, Jesus is the only prophet who was believed in while He was still in His mother's womb.

Muslim commentators agree that the prophet Yahya (John the Baptist) was the first person to believe that Jesus was the Word of God.

The following story was reported by Al-Razi, a well-known early Muslim scholar:

The mother of Jesus met the mother of Yahya, peace be upon them. Both were pregnant, one with Jesus, the other with Yahya. Yahya's mother said to Mary, "Do you feel I am pregnant?" Mary said, "I am also pregnant." The wife of Zekaraiah said, "I found that he who is inside me bows down to the one inside of you."

Al-Razi explains, "This is what is meant by John's confirming (or believing in) the Word of God which is Jesus, found in the Qur'an, Surah 3:39. It reads: 'Yahya witnessing the truth of a word from Allah.'"[3]

Yahya Bowed Down to Jesus According to Reliable Islamic Records

Abdullah Ibn Abbas (see appendix) gained the reputation of being the most informed person among the Muslim people as to what God revealed to Muhammad. Ibn Abbas made known that the appropriate response to Jesus as the Word of God is *to bow down to Him* and that the prophet Yahya was the first to acknowledge that Jesus is the Word of God. Ibn Abbas says, "His [Yahya's] bowing down to Jesus in His mother's womb was his expression of faith in Jesus."[4]

Ibn Abbas further states: "Yahya's bowing down in his mother's womb is his believing that Jesus is the Word of God."[5] Ibn Abbas noted that Yahya was the first to believe and confirm that Jesus is "the Word of God" and "His Spirit."[6]

It is amazing to read of early Muslims believing that *Yahya bowed down to Jesus*, because Yahya was an eminent prophet according to the Qur'an and the Bible.

Bowing Down Is a Clear Form of Worship

My dear Muslim friend, bowing down is a clear and strong form of worship. Worship is due only to God, who has no partner or equal. The Bible agrees that Jesus is worthy to receive worship because He alone is the eternal, uncreated, divine Word of God. My Muslim friend, God Himself wants us to know that Jesus is His eternal Word and worthy to be worshiped.

Yahya's Heart Was Made Alive, According to Islamic Scholars

In addition, the great Muslim scholar Al-Razi explained why the prophet Yahya was given his name. The name *Yahya* is taken from the verb "to be alive." Al-Razi writes: "Yahya was the first to believe in Jesus, so his heart became alive by that faith."[7]

Only God and His Word can cause a person to be spiritually alive.

Who Is Worthy to Receive Worship, Jesus or Adam?

We read in the Qur'an that after God created Adam, He commanded the angels to bow down before Adam. "And behold, we said to the angels, 'bow down to Adam' and they bowed down" (Surah 2:34; see also 7:11; 15:28–29; 17:61; 18:50; 20:116).

The more you read the facts I presented to you in this book and seek God to reveal the truth to you, the more I am sure that you will discover that, according to all the evidence, only Jesus Christ is worthy to receive this honor.

Every Knee Shall Bow Before Jesus

The Gospel informs us of Jesus' place of honor: "God exalted him [Jesus] to the highest place and gave him the name that is above every name, that at the name of Jesus every knee should bow, in heaven and on earth and under the earth, and every tongue acknowledge that Jesus Christ is Lord, to the glory of God the Father" (Philippians 2:9–11).

My dear friend, the way to know God personally, which I am sharing with you in this book, is not limited to one special people group. Understanding and personally applying this truth is available to all!

JESUS RECEIVES WORSHIP

One of my Muslim friends commented that Jesus never said, "I am God. Worship Me."

Part of my answer was, "Jesus knew if He made this statement many people would accuse Him of blasphemy and His statement would only result in negative impact. The important thing is not whether Jesus made this particular statement or not, but did He talk like He was God? Did He act like He's God? Did He give us enough evidence to conclude that He is God manifested in human flesh? Certainly He did!" For example, after Jesus appeared to Thomas, one of His disciples, and gave him proof of His resurrection and triumph over death, Thomas said to Jesus, "My Lord and my God!" Jesus then did not rebuke Thomas but commended him (John 20:24–29).

Jesus' real identity is established by the unique features of His life, His actions, His miracles, and His words. For example, Jesus promised: "For where two or three gather together as my followers, I am there among them" (Matthew 18:20 NLT).

The Bible documents Jesus receiving worship on many occasions. Here are five instances from the Gospel according to Matthew:

- When wise men followed the star to the child, they "bowed down and worshiped him" and presented gifts (Matthew 2:8–11).
- Jesus was worshiped by a leper He cleansed (Matthew 8:2).
- When Jesus walked on water and the wind ceased, the disciples "worshiped him saying, 'Truly you are the Son of God'" (Matthew 14:33).
- The mother of Zebedee's sons came to Jesus, "kneeling down" (Matthew 20:20).
- Some of the disciples "worshiped him" after His resurrection, on a mountain in Galilee (Matthew 28:16–17).

Three more instances where Jesus received worship in other Gospel accounts are listed below:

- A woman "fell at his feet" and asked Jesus to cast the unclean spirit out of her daughter and He did so (Mark 7:25–30).
- When Jesus ascended into heaven, His disciples "worshiped him" (Luke 24:51–52).
- After Jesus opened the eyes of the man born blind, the man said, "'Lord, I believe,' and he worshiped him" (John 9:32–38).

For additional references to the fact that Jesus received worship see John 20:28, Matthew 9:18, Matthew 28:9, and Luke 5:8.

Note that in all of the instances when Jesus was worshiped, He never refused worship. Not once did Jesus rebuke those who worshiped Him. Although Jesus taught that God was the only one to be worshiped, Jesus permitted people to worship Him.

29

GOD IS LOVE

God is love. The glorious revelation in the Bible is that God loves every single person unconditionally. Every person can know God personally and experience His love and salvation!

PARABLE OF THE LOST PRODIGAL SON

The Qur'an states that God does not love prodigals or "wasters" (Surah 6:141; 7:31). A different picture in the Gospel shows God's astonishing love even for prodigals who are recklessly wasteful. In Luke 15, Jesus teaches the parable of the lost prodigal son and his older brother. Jesus first describes the insulting actions of the younger son, who decided to leave the family farm and asked his father for his share of the inheritance.

The father decided to give his son the choice of staying or leaving. The rebellious son took the money, left his father's house, and went far away to squander the wealth in wild living. But when a famine occurred, he ran out of money. The parable then reads:

When he [the prodigal son] came to his senses, he said, "How many of my father's hired servants have food to spare, and here I am starving to death! I will set out and go back to my father and say to him: Father, I have sinned against heaven and against you. I am no longer worthy to be called your son; make me like one of your hired servants." So he got up and went to his father.

But while he was still a long way off, his father saw him and was filled with compassion for him; he ran to his son, threw his arms around him and kissed him.

The son said to him, "Father, I have sinned against heaven and against you. I am no longer worthy to be called your son."

But the father said to his servants, "Quick! Bring the best robe and put it on him. Put a ring on his finger and sandals on his feet. Bring the fattened calf and kill it. Let's have a feast and celebrate. For this son of mine was dead and is alive again; he was lost and is found." So they began to celebrate.

Meanwhile, the older son was in the field. When he came near the house, he heard music and dancing. So he called one of the servants and asked him what was going on. "Your brother has come," he replied, "and your father has killed the fattened calf because he has him back safe and sound."

The older brother became angry and refused to go in. So his father went out and pleaded with him. But he answered his father, "Look! All these years I've been slaving for you and never disobeyed your orders. Yet you never gave me even a young goat so I could celebrate with my friends. But when this son of yours who has squandered your property with prostitutes comes home, you kill the fattened calf for him!"

"My son," the father said, "you are always with me, and everything I have is yours. But we had to celebrate and be glad, because this brother of yours was dead and is alive again; he was lost and is found." (Luke 15:17–32)

The older brother symbolizes the "religious" person who never really experienced what it meant to be a son, or appreciated the thoughts and feelings of his loving father. He served his father not out of love, but primarily out of a desire for reward. He did not have genuine love for his brother or his father. He deserved to be punished for being mean and selfish; however, the father displayed grace by lovingly pleading with him to join the feast.

This parable could also be called "The Parable of the Loving Father." During this time apart, the father was most likely grieving as he thought about his son living without the love and comfort of his family. The father was suffering deeply because he felt that his son was hurting. In the Jewish culture of the first century, a respectable old man would not run out to meet his disloyal son who had brought disgrace to his family and village. Yet the father in the parable *did* run out to welcome his son because he loved him passionately and he naturally demonstrated his love. It did not matter to him that many of the people in the village would ridicule him, for the father had never ceased to love his son. He still loved him even when the son was squandering his inheritance in wild living. Had the father insisted on judging his younger son according to his works, this story would have ended with a funeral instead of a celebration!

Even though the prodigal son's sin broke his relationship with his father, the father did not ask him to *earn* his forgiveness. Jesus is teaching us in this parable that God's love for each one of us is never rooted in our worthiness, but rather in His own nature. We are accepted by grace alone! Certainly Jesus is teaching that God's love is undeserved. God loves sinners and eagerly awaits their return. The heavenly Father patiently waits for the return of even the worst sinners because He loves people regardless of their own unworthiness. God, as described in the Bible, does not love only those who love Him. God demonstrated His inexhaustible love in action—and that demonstration was costly. My Muslim friend, God knows you completely and loves you unconditionally.

PERFECT WORSHIP THAT PLEASES GOD

What is the perfect form of worship our Creator desires we give Him? Is it the mere performance of religious duties? Fasting, praying, giving some of our money, reading God's Word, going to our place of worship, etc.? Of course, this is not the most perfect form of worship. God knows that it is possible for someone to perform all these religious duties and at the same time not have a heart and mind dedicated to God.

Believers can try to obey God and serve Him out of wrong motives, such as fear, habit, pride, or prospect of reward. God knows that our mere performance of religious duties does not necessarily mean that we are surrendering or submitting our lives completely to Him.

Love God

Jesus revealed to us the perfect form of worship that God desired we give Him. Matthew, one of Jesus' disciples, recorded in chapter 22 that a Jewish man asked Jesus: "Teacher, which is the greatest commandment in the Law?" Jesus replied: "Love the Lord your God with all your heart and with all your soul and with all your mind" (vv. 36–37). Jesus taught us that loving God with our whole being is what God desires of us in worshiping

Him. Jesus also taught us that if we truly love God we will express our love through obeying Him.

In the Injeel (Gospel) God is not just asking us to obey Him, but He is asking us first to fall in love with Him, and as a natural result of loving Him, we will want to obey His commandments.

Loving God the way Jesus taught us is the perfect form of worship because it means giving Him our emotions, our thoughts, our will, and our goals and living to please Him every day of our lives.

TWO QUESTIONS

Now we need to answer two important questions:

1. Is it possible for a believer to give God this perfect form of worship?
2. Is God worthy to receive such love?

In other words, who is this God that asks me to give Him my life and love Him supremely?

Is it possible for the Muslim believer to wholeheartedly love God?

Answering this question depends on understanding three important issues:

(1) What is the relationship between the believer and God?

According to the Qur'an, God is the Master, and the believer is treated only as a slave (abd). We read in Surah 19:93, "Not one of the beings in heaven and the earth but must come to Allah most gracious as a Abd (slave)."

A slave or servant works to earn a place in his master's house. The slave does not work because he loves his master but primarily for his own benefits and rewards.

I remember when I was a child, my parents had a servant. One of her duties was to make sure that I went to sleep in bed at a certain time. In order to make me fall asleep quickly so she could go and watch TV, she would tell me a scary story, saying that the bogey man or evil spirit would come to my room if I didn't fall asleep right away. I do not think she really loved me or loved my parents. For years I was afraid to be in a dark room alone. I think I am still traumatized by this experience (just kidding!).

Performance of Religious Duties

According to Islam, God's acceptance of the believer is conditional upon the Muslim's performance of religious duties. However, even if the believer lived all his or her life trying to perform all the religious duties, nevertheless, Allah still has the right to dismiss the believer and not accept the believer in heaven. This is because Allah is the master and believers are just slaves.

When I was a child growing up in Egypt, I remember becoming friends with one of the servants hired by my parents. He fixed my bicycle many times. We played soccer on the same team, and he would climb trees to pick fruits and give them to me.

One day I heard my parents talking on the balcony. They had decided to dismiss my servant friend and send him back to his village. I cried and told my parents he was doing a good job. They answered me, "Why are you crying, Samy, and getting emotional? He is just a servant."

You see, this relationship of slave or servant with his master is not conducive to heartfelt love. Genuine love cannot come from or to a servant or slave mentality.

We read in Surah 23:6 of "Those who dispense their charity with their hearts full of fear because they will return to their Lord." Aisha, one of Muhammad's wives, asked Muhammad, "Oh apostle of God, is the one who is afraid of God the one who commits adultery, steals, drinks wine, thus he is afraid of punishment?" Muhammad told her, "No, oh daughter of Sedik, he is the one who prays, fasts and gives alms, thus he is afraid that God may not accept these things from him."[1]

Unpredictable Judge

The Qur'an describes God as an unpredictable judge. Surah 14:14 states: "Allah leads astray those whom He pleases and guides whom He pleases." In the Qur'an, God never promises complete forgiveness of the believer's sins. He does not guarantee believers' eternal life with him in paradise except if they were killed fighting the enemy of God.

Abu Bakr was one of Muhammad's closest companions. Muslims believe him to be the most exalted person after the prophets. He was elected to be the Muslim leader (Caliph) after Muhammad's death. But he was frightened about his own eternal destiny. In *Teachings of Islam*, in the chapter entitled "Fear of Allah," he was quoted as saying: "Oh bird! How lucky you are! You eat, you drink and fly under the shade of the trees and you fear no reckoning of the Day of Judgment! I wish I were just like you."[2]

Abu Bakr also said: "I swear to God that I do not feel safe from God's cunning (deceitfulness) even if one of my feet is already inside paradise."[3] When resurrection, paradise, or hell was mentioned in his presence, Abu Bakr said: "I wish I were a tree eaten by an animal; I wish I had never been born."[4] Obviously he was frightened of God.

Umar, a very close companion to Muhammad, was elected to be the second leader (Caliph) of the Muslim world. He was highly exalted by Muhammad and all Muslim scholars. We read in *Teachings of Islam*, one of the most popular Islamic records, that when the Muslims were very weak in the beginning of Islam, the prophet Muhammad prayed to Allah to strengthen the Muslims with Umar's Islam.[5] Yet Umar, also scared of hell, would often hold a straw in his hand and say, "I wish I were a straw like this." And sometimes he would say, "I wish my mother had not given birth to me."[6]

Who Is Going to Hell?

We read in the Qur'an that God said: "If we had so willed we could certainly have brought every soul its true guidance. But the word from me will come true. I will fill hell with jinns and men all together" (Surah 32:13). Muhammad said: "By Allah, though I am the Apostle of Allah, yet I do not know what Allah will do to me."[7]

Muhammad frequently prayed, "O Allah, I seek refuge with you from the punishment in the grave and from the punishment in the hell fire and from the affliction of life and death."[8] As you can see, God as described in Islam is indeed a frightful God who cannot be trusted. Even the most devout person cannot feel safe with Him.

We read in the Qur'an about God that "He forgives whom He pleases and tortures whom He pleases" (Surah 5:18). Therefore, it is impossible for sinners, guilty people (notice that all people including believers are sinners), to develop feelings of love toward a judge like that. As soon as the Muslim believer discovers a verse like that in the Qur'an, he becomes frightened of God.

Again, you can see from the description of God's relationship with the believer in Islam that this relationship is not conducive to heartfelt love.

Frightened of Hell

The description of God in Islam causes the Muslim person to be frightened of God's wrath and eternal punishment in hell. This makes the Muslim's love toward God self-motivated. Thus everything the Muslim does for God, deep down in his mind, he is doing for himself. The Muslim believer, therefore, cannot truly love God for God's sake, for who He is, but for his own sake in order to reduce God's wrath and to gain God's forgiveness and acceptance.

No Genuine Love

Thus, the Muslim believer's love toward God cannot be genuine. Genuine love must be the exercise of the purest affections of the heart toward God. Naturally, God desires a willing response of love from those who worship Him.

(2) Did God manifest His love toward us?

Our love toward God is a response to His love toward us. The second thing that must exist before the believer is able to love God is this: The believer needs to see God express His love for him or her. Of course it is natural that our expressions of love toward God can only be in response to and in gratitude for the manifestation of God's love toward us. Only the believer who sees and understands a demonstration of God's fervent love toward him or her will respond in love toward God. The greater God's expression of His love toward us, the stronger our response will be.

The Qur'an never said that God loves every living person and that God desires to enter into a loving relationship with the people He created. The Qur'an never states that God pursues sinful people and seeks to save them and to fellowship with them. The Qur'an does not tell us of any great act of love that God did in the history of His dealings with mankind. We find no evidence in the Qur'an that God has feelings of love, deep affection, toward sinners or even toward believers. Therefore, it is impossible for the Muslim believer to wholeheartedly love God.

(3) Can we experience God's love?

This is the third thing that must exist before the believer is able to love God. Not only does the believer need to see God strongly express His love for him or her, but the believer also needs to feel love in his or her heart toward God. For example, a man can express his love to a woman, buy her nice things, say loving words, then ask her, "How do you feel about us?" And she can say, "I appreciate that you love me and how nice you are to me, but I would like us to be just friends. I do not feel that I am in love with you. I do not have that thing for you."

Ninety-nine Names Given to God

According to Muslim scholars, there are ninety-nine beautiful names given to God in the Qur'an—names such as the Powerful, the Judge, the Sovereign, Eternal, Merciful, etc. It is significant to notice that none of these names is "the Loving" (in Arabic that would be Al Muhub). God is called "the Merciful" about one hundred times in the Qur'an, but He is never called "the Loving" even one time.

One of the greatest Muslim theologians in Islamic history, Al-Ghazzali, explains God's love as consisting solely of objective acts of kindness and expressions of approval. He denies that God feels any love in his own heart toward mankind. Al-Ghazzali states: "God remains above the feeling of love."[9]

Al-Ghazzali confirms this unfortunate teaching in the Qur'an by describing God's love: "Love and mercy are desired in respect of their objects only for the sake of their fruit and benefit and not because of empathy or feeling."[10] In other words, when God says He loves you, what He means is He will show mercy to you by giving you good things, but you cannot interpret that to mean He feels anything in His heart for you. This is not good, especially because love is much stronger, richer, and deeper than mercy.

You can show mercy to a poor person by giving him a few dollars or something to eat. On the other hand, a father's love for his children motivates him to sacrifice for them. Love is the greatest virtue that anyone could ever have.

It is significant to know that these ninety-nine names given to God in the Qur'an are not part of God's essential being. According to Islam and Muslim scholars, God can express or withhold them at will. They are no more than occasional characteristics of God. Allah can choose to be faithful, loving, forgiving, or merciful toward someone and/or he can choose to be unforgiving and unmerciful toward another person.

Subjective Love

Because God as described in Islam is empty of subjective love toward believers, Muslim believers cannot feel or experience God's love in their hearts. Therefore, no Muslim is able to develop within his or her being feelings of love toward God, especially from all the heart, soul, and mind. The God whom the Qur'an describes does not satisfy the thirst and longing of our hearts and souls. It is like a certain woman who loved a man, wanted to marry him, spend the rest of her life with him, and devote herself to him. Unfortunately, this man refused to let her know that he loved her. He never told her, "I love you." He told her, "I cannot promise you that you will be with me for the rest of my life." He refused to marry her. But he bestowed gifts on her when she pleased and obeyed him—as a way to reward her and express his approval to her. He wanted her to be only his servant, his slave.

If you were that woman, how would you feel? Would you feel loved? Would your heart be full of love for this man? Likewise, it is impossible for Muslims to give God the most perfect form of worship, which again is to love God with all their heart, soul, and mind. They are unable to have and to express such love to God through joyful, willing submission to His commandments.

The Qur'an acknowledges that Allah is closer than one's jugular vein; at the same time it also describes Him as very distant, so unreachable and inaccessible.

Please compare what I just shared with you with what the Bible teaches regarding these three important topics:

Is it possible for the Christian believer to wholeheartedly love God?

(1) First, God declared in the Bible that He desires to draw so close to us as a loving father would draw near to his children. Jesus instructed His disciples, when praying to God, to call on Him as our Father (Matthew 6:9).

We now from the Gospel that the moment you repent and put your faith in Jesus that He died to pay the penalty for all the wrong you have done, a miracle will happen to you: you will be born through God's Spirit and become a child of God. We read in the Gospel (Injeel), "But to all who believed him [Jesus] and accepted him, he gave the right to become children of God" (John 1:12 NLT).

Jesus told His disciples, "The Father himself loves you" (John 16:27). This brings about a relationship that is conducive to love.

GOD'S PARENTAL LOVE

I remember one day I saw a couple of my extended family members holding their newborn baby. I noticed their strong attachment and affection toward their baby. They said to me: "Samy, look how beautiful, gorgeous our baby is." I was too distracted by the crying, spitting, and smell of the baby. Obviously, the parents appreciated the beauty of their baby much more than I did. I did not share their feelings. To them, their baby was the most precious, beautiful person in the world.

Through what I saw of the parents' love for their newborn baby, God showed me that He loves me, in spite of my imperfections, much more than these parents could ever love their baby. I could feel God saying to me, "Even though I love every living person, Samy, you are my child. You are much more special to Me than the people who haven't yet become My children. I know all your mistakes, past failures, and present weaknesses and shortcomings. Regardless of anything not perfect in you, you are My most treasured and precious possession. Samy, you are born of My Spirit and you are My child!"

We read in the Bible: "See what great love the Father has lavished on us, that we should be called children of God! And that is what we are!" (1 John 3:1). Because God is pleased to adopt us and care for us as His children and becomes our very own Father, this must mean that He is willing to enter into a deep and personal relationship with us. Now His command to love Him has the best prospect of fulfillment.

We Are Going to Heaven

Of course we know that God is the judge of all the earth, but if we know God only as Judge, we will be scared when we think about that day when His righteous judgment will be revealed.

269

But we no longer anticipate a judge on the throne of justice before whom we should be condemned to eternal damnation for our sins. We know God as our loving heavenly Father. While He may in love and with the purpose of correction chastise us as His children (when needed), it is love and forgiveness that really characterize the relationship between Him and us.

I love God's Word: "There is no fear in love. But perfect love drives out fear, because fear has to do with punishment. The one who fears is not made perfect in love" (1 John 4:18). These words simply mean that anyone who has no deep assurance in his heart that his sins are forgiven will fear God. And if fear of God's eternal punishment in hell exists in a man's heart, he cannot develop true love toward God. Since we are God's children, we are sure that God will never send us to spend eternity in hell or even put us there for one day.

The Bible assures us: "We are God's children. Now if we are children, then we are heirs—heirs of God and co-heirs with Christ" (Romans 8:16–17). Through Christ we will always be God's children. While a servant must work to earn his place in his master's home, usually must sleep in a different place, and can be fired at any time, a son cannot be dismissed. That which is the father's is the child's also.

My Personal Story

I was working as a defense lawyer in my father's legal firm in Egypt. I was living a comfortable life because my father was very rich. He was a famous defense lawyer and owned many real estate properties. But I was not happy—I had a serious conflict: Most of my clients were drug dealers, and all of them were guilty. I was making good money, but I was helping drug dealers get out of prison. I was not living for God but for myself. My goal was to be successful. God spoke to me through the Bible in the book of

Hebrews (chapter 11) and through the life of Moses. God called me to leave Egypt and come to America and live by faith. God convinced me that it is better to suffer for the sake of Christ than to own the treasures of Egypt.

When I told my father my decision to go to America, he said: "Samy, why do you want to leave? Don't you know that one day, my son, everything I have will be yours? It will be my joy to give you what I own."

Likewise, we read Jesus' beautiful words to us in the Gospel (Injeel): "Do not be afraid, little flock, for your Father has been pleased to give you the kingdom" (Luke 12:32). We look to God as our heavenly Father. We know now that His kingdom will be our future home. No fear here of a master whose acceptance we have to strive to obtain. Muslims strive all their lives to gain the favor of God. We as true believers and followers of Christ begin with God's favor imprinted on our hearts. We begin where Muslims hope to end.

We rejoice now in our knowledge and experience as children of God, that when our time on earth ends, we will be with God forever, sharing His kingdom. Because we are God's children, we now feel the most irresistible attraction toward God.

God's Awesome Revelation of His love

(2) Second we read in the Gospel: "God is love" (1 John 4:8). Love is the most prevalent characteristic revealed about God in the Bible. God's heart is full of emotions of love for you and for me, and for the whole human race—including sinners. We read in the Bible, "God our Savior . . . wants all people to be saved" (1 Timothy 2:3–4).

I often ask my Muslim friends: "In what way has God shown His love for you?" They usually respond: "God has given me health, family, life, a job, etc." While we feel grateful for everything we have that God gave us, we as followers of Jesus Christ have the strongest, most perfect proof of God's love for us. It is not health or wealth. Jesus said: "God so loved the world that he gave his one and only Son, that whoever believes in him shall not perish but have eternal life" (John 3:16).

I already explained in chapters 14 and 27 that according to the facts we agree about in the Qur'an and the Bible, Jesus could not have been called anything other than the "Son of God." I also proved throughout section three in this book that as Abraham's willingness to sacrifice his son for God proved that he had perfect sacrificial love toward God and that he loved God more than anything; likewise, the Bible declares: "God demonstrates his own love for us in this: While we were still sinners, Christ died for us" (Romans 5:8). When Abraham obeyed God and was about to sacrifice his son, he proved he was willing to give God everything and anything. There was nothing more precious to his heart than his son. Likewise, God revealed to us in the Bible His awesome heart of love and perfect intentions toward us. We read: "He who did not spare his own Son, but gave him up for us all—how will he not also, along with him, graciously give us all things?" (Romans 8:32).

Not only do we see God's passionate love in the gift of His Son for us, but we also see His love because of who Jesus is and what He said: "Anyone who has seen me has seen the Father" (John 14:9). We see in Jesus the very personification of God's passionate love toward us. This awesome love that Jesus fully expressed in His life and death was nothing more or less than God's own love for us. Remember, Jesus came to die for sinners (Mark 2:17). In Jesus, God's expression of love toward you and me and toward all sinners cannot be improved upon or matched. God revealed His passionate love for me in a way that causes me and motivates me to fall in love with Him from all my heart.

We Can Experience God's Love

(3) Third, God in the Bible does not only give us the most powerful expressions of His love that we can see, but He also gave us the most real experience of this love that we can feel. We read in the Bible: "We know how dearly God loves us, because he has given us the Holy Spirit to fill our hearts with his love" (Romans 5:5 NLT). The planting of God's love in our hearts must lead to the motivation of love toward God. God told us in the Bible: "Because we are his children, God has sent the Spirit of his Son into our hearts, prompting us to call out, 'Abba, Father'" (Galatians 4:6 NLT).

Through the Holy Spirit who is given to every true believer in Jesus Christ, we are able to actually experience God's love for us within our souls and hearts.

God sent the Spirit of His Son into our hearts to make us conscious, right within our being, that God is our loving heavenly Father. We read in the Bible: "So you have not received a spirit that makes you fearful slaves. Instead, you received God's Spirit when he adopted you as his own children. Now we call him 'Abba, Father.' For his Spirit joins with our spirit to affirm that we are God's children" (Romans 8:15–16 NLT).

I like to tell my Muslim friends: "If you put your trust in God to save you, through the sacrifice of Jesus Christ, God will draw so near to you—just like a father adopting a child and then taking him in his arms." Please allow me to share another story with you.

A man decided to adopt a child. He signed all the necessary papers and filled out the forms. The adoption was approved and legally recognized. Then he went to the orphanage and took the child with him to his home. He asked the child: "Do you see this room? This is your room. Do you see all these toys? These are your toys. This is your house, and I am your father who loves you." Then he took the child in his arms and gave him a big, warm hug.

Imagine how precious this child felt in these wonderful moments.

You too, my Muslim friend, will have the most wonderful experience of God's love when the Holy Spirit enters your life and you become a child of God. The Holy Spirit who indwells us has given us the definite knowledge now that we are God's beloved children and that our place in His eternal kingdom is an absolute certainty.

The love of the heavenly Father made manifest in Jesus Christ becomes a reality that we feel in our hearts and lives through the Holy Spirit—whom God placed within our hearts. (Incidentally, have you noticed the triune nature of God here?) God dwells in us; we are united to God; His Spirit dwells in our being. We read in the Bible: "And he has identified us as his own by placing the Holy Spirit in our hearts as the first installment that guarantees everything he has promised us" (2 Corinthians 1:22 NLT).

We are joined to God in a relationship that can never be broken. The Holy Spirit within us is like a deposit that guarantees our inheritance until we acquire possession of it. "The Spirit is God's guarantee that he will give us the inheritance he promised and that he has purchased us to be his own people. He did this so we would praise and glorify him" (Ephesians 1:14 NLT). The seal of God is upon us. Because I can experience God's love for me, I wholeheartedly fall in love with God.

CONCLUSION

It is clear that the Bible contains the true, full revelation of God. First, according to the Qur'an, God only requires believers to perform some religious duties. However, only Jesus has revealed to us the will of God regarding the perfect form of worship that God desires we give Him. Jesus said the greatest commandment is to love God with all your heart, soul, and mind.

Certainly Jesus' words revealed the will of God because there is no higher or better form of worship that we can give God than to love Him from our whole being. And it certainly makes sense that the Creator of the universe deserves to receive this perfect form of worship from us, His creation.

Second, the God whom the Gospel reveals to us has the most wonderful character and heart. He is absolutely perfect:

a) He passionately reveals His magnificent love for us through Jesus' life, words, and death on the cross.
b) He made it possible for us to become His adopted children through faith in Jesus.
c) He made it possible for us to feel and experience His fatherly love within our hearts through the Holy Spirit who indwells us.

It certainly makes sense that God, our Creator, has the most loving heart and wonderful, perfect character. Only the Bible reveals this awesome character.

Third, God as Jesus revealed Him made it possible for us to give Him perfect worship as our natural response to what God has done for us, and is doing for us right now, and shall do for us forever as His children. The true believer of Jesus can sincerely tell God, "There is no limit to the potential of my love for You. I want to love You, seek You, obey You, serve You, and know You every day of my life."

I can genuinely and easily say: "I am in love with God. God is worthy of my thoughts, affections, emotions, and my life. God, as Jesus revealed Him, made it possible for me to willingly and joyfully submit my life to Him and obey Him. When I think about God and spend some time with Him, I find myself drawn to Him with the most irresistible attraction. God's love captures my heart." I can agree with the apostle Paul when he said: "Christ's love controls us" (2 Corinthians 5:14 NLT).

God's love compels me to forget myself and joyfully submit my life, even as a slave in God's hand. I become His slave not to get something from Him, not out of fear of Him, but because I fell in love with Him. As I mentioned, I grew up in a rich family in Egypt. I used to ask my parents to do or buy things for me. Then God called me to go to America in 1980.

I remember that after I came to America, my parents came to visit me every year. They would ask me, "What would you like us to bring you?" In the first few years I used to ask for money, clothes, certain food items, etc. After I lived in America alone for a few years, I had a chance to appreciate their love toward me as I thought about the generous way they treated me. The care, the love they gave me—they did everything perfect parents could have done for their son. After a few years I realized their strong love toward me, and I fell in love with them in a much deeper way. So they asked me again: "We are coming in a couple of months. What do you want us to bring you?" I replied: "I do not want you to bring me anything. I just want to spend time with you, and I would like to take you to wonderful places in America—like Disneyland, the beach, and parks. Father, I'd like to take you to a jacuzzi."

I realized that in the same way, God's love toward me changed me and is changing me every day; I fall in love with Him more deeply every day, more than the day before, and my greatest desire now is to please Him.

A WORD FROM MY HEART

Through faith in Jesus Christ we have been forgiven by God, we have come to enjoy a living relationship with God, we have received the Spirit of God in our hearts, and we have been adopted by God as His eternal children. He destined us to share His kingdom. You, too, can have a living relationship with God. You can experience Him as your loving heavenly Father. You can enjoy His forgiveness right now. And you can be assured of His divine presence in your life and can be certain that heaven is your home and destiny.

The fatherly love of God for you, my dear Muslim friend, is unsurpassed. The moment you accept Jesus as your Savior, you will be spiritually born again, and you will experience the heavenly Father's loving arms drawing you to His bosom. Then you will find yourself drawn to Him with the most irresistible attraction. You will fall in love with Him from the depth of your being!

My precious Muslim reader, I beg you, do not strive all your life to try to gain the favor of God. Right now, you can begin enjoying God's favor in the depth of your heart by simply placing yourself in the position to receive it:

1. Admit that you are a sinner.
2. Repent of your sins; decide not to live in sin anymore. (*toba* in Arabic)
3. Put your faith in Jesus Christ as your personal Savior from sin and its penalty.
4. This is your testimony (*shahada* in Arabic) that Jesus is your Savior.

30

JESUS IS UNIQUE BECAUSE HE IS OUR SAVIOR

The Bible teaches that we are all separated from God as sinners in need of the Savior. We all need to be reconciled to God.

SINNERS NEED THE SAVIOR

The problem is that sin is an integral part of our human nature. All kinds of iniquity dwell in the human heart, such as lust, envy, greed, pride, hatred, selfishness, and dishonesty. These sins and others have vicious control within each person; they make all humans captive to the power of sin and its ongoing temptations.

JESUS WON THE BATTLE AGAINST SATAN AND SIN

The Gospel tells us that Jesus, the only One who is pure from sin, came "in the likeness of sinful flesh" and "he condemned sin in the flesh" (Romans 8:3). He lived without committing one single sin. Jesus had complete victory over all of Satan's temptations. Jesus' divine nature guaranteed His victory in the battle against Satan and sin. Jesus won the battle on our behalf. The awesome news of the Gospel is that Jesus came and defeated the power of sin in its own dwelling place inside the human body.

You Can Be Free from the Love and Power of Sin

The wonderful news of the Gospel is that God made it possible for you to be united with Jesus through His Spirit, who will reside within you at the very moment you place your faith in Jesus as your Savior. As a natural consequence of being united with Jesus, you will enjoy the fruits of His victory. You can experience freedom from the slavery to sin for the first time in your life. Jesus said, "Very truly I tell you, everyone who sins is a slave to sin," and He also said, "If the Son sets you free, you will be free indeed" (John 8:34, 36). We can only be liberated from the bondage of sin by the power of God within us. We cannot be set free by our own willpower.

The gospel's beautiful message is that Jesus came to save you and set you free from the captivity and love of sin. The Savior Jesus Christ came to do what the law and prophets could not do. "The reason the Son of God appeared was to destroy the devil's work" (1 John 3:8).

Jesus warns us, "Unless you believe that I AM who I claim to be, you will die in your sins" (John 8:24 NLT).

You Can Be Saved from the Penalty of Sin

God is just and requires payment for all the offenses (sins) we commit against Him. Jesus made the payment by taking the punishment in our place.

Jesus suffered the most horrible consequence of our sin—

death. By suffering the wrath of God toward sin, Jesus paid for the sin debt of every person.

"Since we have been united with him in his death . . . we know that our old sinful selves were crucified with Christ" (Romans 6:5–6 NLT).

Again, when you believe in Christ and open your heart to receive Him in your life, He will enter your life and you will become united to Christ. As a consequence you will benefit from Christ's death, which paid the penalty for all your sins.

You Can Enjoy God's Forgiveness in Your Heart

When you believe that the penalty for everything wrong you have done is already paid for through Christ, you will be united to Christ and experience and feel within your heart and soul the forgiveness of God for all your sins.

In other words, since Christ already paid the penalty and you are united with Him, you will benefit from what He did for you on the cross. The good news of the Bible is that Jesus came to save you and me and set us free from having to suffer the consequences of everything wrong we have done. The penalty has been paid.

Jesus also can set you free from any guilty feelings or thoughts that exist within you as a consequence of the wrong things you do. You will then enjoy a wonderful peace with God and peace within yourself. And Christ's righteousness will be counted as yours.

You Can Live Forever with God

The glorious news of the Gospel is that Jesus came and conquered death itself. When Jesus bodily rose from the dead and ascended to be with God the Father, He declared victory over death. Jesus reversed the worst consequence of sin, which is eternal separation from God's presence. Because believers in Christ are united with Him, they share in and benefit from Christ's resurrection.

"Since we have been united with him in his death, we will also be raised to life as he was" (Romans 6:5 NLT). Our union with Christ assures our future resurrection from the dead. True believers in Christ will die only physically, and will enjoy eternal life in God's presence forever.

You Can Be Certain That You Are Going to Heaven

You can also be certain within your heart and soul that you are going to heaven. The amazing news of the Gospel is that the moment you believe in Jesus and go to God in repentance, God's Holy Spirit will come to dwell within you, and He will assure you that you are now going to heaven. Paradise will become your home and your destiny. The Gospel declares: "And Christ lives within you, so even though your body will die because of sin, the Spirit gives you life because you have been made right with God. The Spirit of God, who raised Jesus from the dead, lives in you. And just as God raised Christ Jesus from the dead, he will give life to your mortal bodies by this same Spirit living within you" (Romans 8:10–11 NLT).

The reason you will know for sure you are going to heaven is that the same Jesus who lives in heaven will come to live in you now through His eternal Spirit. The living and life-giving Spirit of Christ imparts to you eternal life with God. Jesus declares to us in the Gospel, "Because I live, you also will live" (John 14:19).

Jesus Bridged the Gap between Mankind and God

Jesus fully bridged the gap between heaven and earth. He made it possible for sinful man to be reconciled with the Holy God.

For this reason, Jesus declared, "I am the way and the truth and the life. No one comes to the Father except through me" (John 14:6).

Jesus Satisfies Our Spiritual Thirst

Jesus knows that you need a genuine friend to depend on. Jesus would like to be your perfect Friend. Jesus told His disciples, "I no longer call you slaves . . . you are my friends" (John 15:14–15 NLT).

Jesus said, "I have come that they may have life, and have it to the full" (John 10:10). God created us in such a way that we will never be satisfied or enjoy life fully until we have the right relationship with Him through faith in Jesus.

Jesus can satisfy our deepest spiritual and emotional longing. He said, "I am the bread of life. Whoever comes to me will never go hungry, and whoever believes in me will never be thirsty" (John 6:35).

Jesus knows that you are like a traveler wandering through the desert of life. You are hungry for love and peace, thirsty for joy and happiness and are looking for it everywhere without success. Christ promises you that if you go to Him, believing in Him and following His teachings, this deep longing will be satisfied forever. When you believe in Christ, He will be like cold water to your thirsty soul.

"Jesus stood and said in a loud voice, 'Let anyone who is thirsty come to me and drink'" (John 7:37).

God is inviting you to a life of joy despite any adverse circumstances you may face. Jesus said, "I have told you this so that my joy may be in you and that your joy may be complete" (John 15:11).

WHAT IS YOUR DECISION?

Jesus speaks to all people through the Gospel. He speaks to you, my Muslim friend, because He loves you. Jesus promised,

"Come to me, all you who are weary and burdened, and I will give you rest" (Matthew 11:28).

Jesus wants to guide you and help you discover the purpose of your life. "When Jesus spoke again to the people, he said, 'I am the light of the world. Whoever follows me will never walk in darkness, but will have the light of life'" (John 8:12).

Jesus offers eternal life to you and to me. "Most assuredly, I say to you, he who believes in Me has everlasting life" (John 6:47 NKJV).

God's Supreme Love Draws Us to Him

My dear friend, I urge you to believe God's Word and take a step by faith. I know from personal experience that the moment you believe in Jesus as your Lord and Savior, you, too, will actually experience and taste within your heart and soul God's great and wonderful love for you. God wants to make you satisfied. He desires to fill your life with joy, love, hope, and peace. God desires to have fellowship with you. God is speaking to you right now saying, "I have loved you with an everlasting love; I have drawn you with unfailing kindness" (Jeremiah 31:3).

Jesus declares, "For God so loved the world that he gave his one and only Son, that whoever believes in him shall not perish but have eternal life" (John 3:16).

For God	the greatest Lover
so loved	the greatest degree
the world	the greatest company
that he gave	the greatest act
his one and only Son	the greatest gift (Jesus)
that whoever	the greatest opportunity
believes	the greatest simplicity

in him	the greatest attraction
shall not perish	the greatest promise
but	the greatest difference
have	the greatest certainty
eternal life	the greatest possession!

My friend, our loving God is longing to have a personal relationship with you. He chose *you*—now the choice is *yours*.

Your joy now and your eternal happiness depend on your decision. If you choose to put your faith in Jesus as your Savior, here is a suggested personal and specific prayer. Pray it if you mean it with all your heart.

Thank You, Jesus, for dying on the cross to pay the penalty for my sins. I need You to come into my life and be my Savior.

God, I do not want to live far from You any longer. I am sorry for everything I have done wrong. I ask You to forgive me because of what Jesus has done for me. I want to experience Your love and do Your will. In Jesus' name, Amen.

After you prayed this prayer, please contact me and let me know. I would like to congratulate you on having made the best and most important decision of your life—to receive the miracle of eternal life with God!

Your New Life Walking with God

My dear brother or sister in Christ, now that you are born again, please pay attention to these important issues:

First, find a church that faithfully teaches God's Word. It is essential to join a church that teaches that one must be born again by the Spirit of God (John 3:3). Please beware of church groups that claim to be "Christian" but do not correctly follow the teachings of the Gospel.

Second, it is important to read the Bible daily. It is the complete, inspired, and reliable Word of God! And remember to spend time in God's presence in prayer so that you will grow spiritually. Talk to God anytime—He is your perfect, loving heavenly Father and best Friend.

Third, before I leave you, I want you to know that while we are on this earth, we will all face difficulties and hard times. However, God promises that He will be with us, and He will cause all things to work together for our good because we love Him (Romans 8:28).

My friend, now you begin your journey of discovering the fruitful, meaningful, and rich life that God created you to live. By walking with God daily through faith you will experience God's promises for you. And you will be able to enjoy the wonderful blessings and marvelous love that God has for you.

Warmly, your servant,

SAMY TANAGHO

Glad News! is also available in Albanian, Arabic, Bosnian, Simplified Chinese and Traditional Chinese, Farsi, French, Romanian, Russian, and Spanish. Other translations are in progress. Please contact Glad News for Muslims Ministry:
PO Box 28961
Santa Ana, CA 92799
(714) 514-2558
www.gladnewsministry.com
e-mail: Samy@gladnewsministry.com

APPENDIX

ABDULLAH IBN ABBAS
(Companion to Muhammad)

According to Islamic records, Abdullah Ibn Abbas attached himself to the service of Muhammad. He was attentive and alert to whatever Muhammad did and said. He became one of Muhammad's most learned companions. Muhammad prayed that Abdullah Ibn Abbas be granted not just knowledge and understanding but also wisdom. Muhammad would often pray: "O Lord, make him acquire a deep understanding of the religion of Islam and instruct him in the meaning and interpretation of things." The Khalifah, Umar Ibn Al-Khattab, often sought his advice on important matters of state and described him as "the young man of maturity." (*Companions of the Prophet #2*, published by MELS, 61 Alexandra Road, Hendon, London, NW42RX. Abdul Wahid Hamid 1995, 1998)

AL-BUKHARI
(RECORDER OF THE HADITH, CONTAINING
MUHAMMAD'S WORDS AND ACTIONS)

Note that we are using the nine-volume translation of the Hadith (by Al-Bukhari) made by Dr. Muhammad Muhsin Khan titled, *The Translation of the Meanings of Sahih Al-Bukhari*, published by Dar AHYA US-Sunnah Al NABAWIYA. This translation is recommended and approved by all Muslim authorities, including the spiritual leaders of Mecca and Medina. The introduction of Dr. Khan's translation (Volume 1) states that it has been unanimously agreed that Imam Bukhari's work is the most authentic of all the other works in Hadith literature put together. The authenticity of Al-Bukhari's work is such that the religious learned scholars of Islam said concerning him: "The most authentic book after the book of Allah [The Qur'an] is Sahih Al-Bukhari" (page 15 of Vol. 1).

BIBLIOGRAPHY

N ote that all Islamic reference books listed below are recognized internationally in the Muslim world. They are republished annually and distributed in Muslim bookstores worldwide.

Abdul-Haqq, Abdiyah Akbar. *Christ in the New Testament and the Qur'an*. Evanston: Abdul-Haqq, 1975.

———. *Sharing Your Faith with a Muslim*. Minneapolis: Bethany Fellowship, 1980.

Abi Hanifah. *Al-Fiqh al-Akbar*. Beirut: Dar al-Kutub al-Elmeyah, 1979.

Al-Ahadith Al-Qudsiyyah. *Divine Narratives*. Translated by Dr. Abdul Khaliqkazi and Dr. Alan B. Day. Tripoli-Lebanon: Dar Al-Iman Publishing House (no date).

Al-Baidawi. *Commentary on the Qur'an*. Beirut: Dar Al-Kotob Al-Ilmiyah, 1999.

Al-Ghazzali. *The Ninety-Nine Beautiful Names of God (AL-Maqsad AL-Asna)*. Translated by David Burrell and Nazih Daher. Cambridge: The Islamic Texts Society, 1992.

Al-Qartaby. *Commentary on the Qur'an*. Beirut: Dar Al-Kotob Al-Ilmiyah, 1996.

Al-Qasemi. *Tafsir (Commentary) of the Holy Qur'an*. Abbreviation to Tafsir Al-Qasemi (Mahasen At.Ta aweel). Beirut: Dar Al-Nafaas, 1993.

Al-Razi. *Tafsir-Al Kabir*, Vol. 3. Beruit: Dar Ehia Al-Tourath Al-Arabi, 1999.

Al-Razi, Fakhr-ul-Din. *Tafsir-Al Kabir*. Beirut: Dar Al-Kutub Al-Ilmiyya, 1990.

Al-Suyuti. *AL-Itqan in Qur'an's Science (AL-Itqan)*. Beirut: Dar Al-Ketab-Al-Araby, 1999.

Alam, Maulana Syed Mohammad Badre. *Descension of Jesus Christ*. Dehli: Dini Book, 1974.

Ali, Abdullah Yusuf. *The Meaning of the Holy Qur'an*, Eighth Edition. Beltsville, MD: Amana Publications, 1996.

Al-Zamkhashri. *The Kash-Shaf*. Beirut: Dar Al-Ketob Al-Elmiyah, 1990.

Anderson, M. *Jesus, the Light and Fragrance of God*, 2 vols. Caney, KS: Pioneer Book Company, 1994.

———. *The Trinity*. Caney, KS: Pioneer Book Company, 1994.

Arberry, A.J. *Revelation and Reason in Islam*. London: George Allen & Unwin Ltd., (no date).

Assfy, Z. *Islam and Christianity*. York, UK: William Sessions Ltd., 1977.

Al-Tabari. *The Book of Religion and Empire*. Lahore, Pakistan: Law Publishing Company.

———. *Commentary on the Qur'an* (Tafsir). Beirut: Dar Al-Kotob- Al-Ilmiyah, 1999.

Bevan, J. *Christianity Explained to Muslims*. Calcutta: YMCA Publishing House, 1952.

Bhai, Abdullah. *AL-Masih—the Anointed One*. Springfield, MO: CMM (no date).

Boice, James Montgomery. *Foundations of the Christian Faith*. Downers Grove, IL: InterVarsity Press, 1981.

Brown, D. *The Divine Trinity, Christianity and Islam*. London: Sheldon Press, 1967.

Bruce, F.F. *The New Testament Documents: Are They Reliable?* Downers Grove, IL: InterVarsity Press, 2000.

Chapman, Colin. *You Go and Do the Same: Studies in Relating to Muslims*. London: CMS, 1983.

Cragg, K. *Jesus and the Muslim*. London: George, Allen and Unwin, 1985.

Crawford, Craig. *The Prophecies: A Journey to the End of Time*. Prophecy Press, 1999.

Durrani, M. H. *The Qur'anic Facts About Jesus*. Karachi, Pakistan: International Islamic Publishers, 1983.

Enns, Paul P. *The Moody Handbook of Theology*. Chicago, IL: Moody, 1989.

Ersen, Ishak. *Jesus Christ in the Traditions of Islam*. Villach, Austria: Light of Life, 1992.

Fadi, Abd Al. *Sin and Atonement in Islam and Christianity*. Beirut: Markaz-ash-Shabiba (no date).

Geisler, Norman and William Nix. *From God To Us: How We Got Our Bible*. Chicago, IL: Moody, 1974.

Ghabril, Nicola Yacob. *Themes for the Diligent: The Good Way*. Rikon, Switzerland (no date).

Gilchrist, John. *The Christian Witness to Muslims*. Roodepoort, Republic of South Africa: Roodepoort Mission Press, 1988.

Goldsack, W. *Christ in Islam*. Madras, India: The Christian Literature Society, 1905.

Guillaume, A. *Life of Muhammad*. A Translation of Ibn Ishaq's Sirat Arasul. London (1955).

The Hadith. CD-ROM. ISL Software Corporation (1996) ALIM.

Hafiz, Sheikh-Ul-Hadith Maualana and Muhammad Zakariyya Kandhalwi. *Teachings of Islam: Stories of the Sahaabah* (rev. trans. of the Urdu book *Hikayat-e-Sahaabah*) Translated by Abdul Rashid Arshad. Library of Islam, Des Plaines, IL (pub. date unknown).

Hahn, E. *Jesus in Islam*. Vaniyamki, India (publishing house not available), (1975).

Halley, Henry. *Halley's Bible Handbook*. Grand Rapids, MI: Zondervan, 2007.

Halverson, Dean C. *The Compact Guide to World Religions*. Minneapolis, MN: Bethany House, 1996.

Hanifah, Imam Abi. *Al-Fiqh al-Akbar*. Beirut: Dar AL-Kutub al-elmeyah, 1997.

Harman, Henry, M. *Introduction to the Study of the Holy Scriptures*, Volume I. New York: Hunt and Eaton, 1878.

Hisham, Ibn, *Al-Sira Al-Nabawiyya.* Beirut: DAR Ibn Hazm.

Hughes, Thomas P. *A Dictionary of Islam*. Lahore, Pakistan: The Premier Book House, 1986.

Imran, Maulana Muhammad. *The Teachings of Jesus in the Light of Al-Qur'an*. Lahore, Pakistan: Malik Sirajudden and Sons, 1980.

Jadeed, Iskander. *Did God Appear in the Flesh?* Rikon, Switzerland: The Good Way (no date).

———. *How to Share the Gospel with Our Muslim Brothers.* Villach, Austria: Light of Life (no date).

———. *The Cross in the Gospel and Qur'an*. Markaz-ash-Shabiba, Beirut (no date).

Jalalan, AL. *Commentary of AL Jalalan* (1983).

Kateregga, Badru D. and David W. Shenk, *A Muslim and a Christian in Dialogue*. Herald Press, PA (1997).

———. *Islam and Christianity*. Kenya: Uzima Press Ltd., 1980.

Khalid, Muhammad Khalid. *The Successor of the Prophet*. Dar Thabet (1986).

Khaliqkazi, Abdul, and A.B. Day, *Al-Ahadith AL-Qudsiyyah*. Tripoli-Lebanon: Dar Al-Iman Publishing House, (no date).

Khan, Muhammad Muhsin. *The Translation of the Meanings of Sahih Al-Bukhari*, 9 vols. Dar Ahya Us-Sunnah (1971).

Kramers, J.H. *Shorter Encyclopedia of Islam*. New York (1961).

Larson, Gary N. *The New Unger's Bible Handbook, Revised*. Chicago: Moody Press, 1984.

Lockyer, Herbert. *All the Messianic Prophecies of the Bible*. Grand Rapids, MI: Zondervan Publishing House, 1973.

Maurer, Andreas. *Illustrations, Parables and Stories*. Mondeor, Republic of South Africa: Mercsa, 1994.

McDowell, Josh. *The New Evidence That Demands a Verdict*. Nashville, TN: Thomas Nelson, 1999.

Morin, Harry. *Responding to Muslims*. Springfield, MO: CMM, 1994.

Morris, Henry M. *Science and the Bible*. Chicago, IL: Moody, 1986.

Nurbakhash, Javad. *Jesus in the Eyes of the Sufis*. London: Khaniqahi-Nimatullahi Publications, 1983.

Obaray, A. H. *Miraculous Conception, Death, Resurrection and Ascension of Jesus as Taught in the Kuran*. Kimberley, Republic of South Africa (1962).

Orethke, J.P. *A Christian Approach to Muslims*. Pasadena, CA: William Carey Library, 1979.

Parrinder, G. *Jesus in the Qur'an*. New York: Oxford University Press, 1977.

Payne, J. Barton, *Encyclopedia of Biblical Prophecy*, 5th ed. Grand Rapids, MI: Baker, 1987.

Pfander, C.G. *Balance of Truth*. Villach, Austria: Light of Life, 1986.

Pickthall, Mohammad Marmaduke. *The Meaning of the Glorious Qur'an*. Dar Ahya US-Sunnah Al-Nabawiya (1930).

Qaradawi, al-Yousef, Elewah Mostafa, and Ali Gammar. *t-Twahid*. Qatar (1968).

Register, R.G. *Dialogue and Interfaith Witness with Muslims*. Chicago, IL: Moody, 1979.

Robertson, K.G. *Jesus or Isa*. New York: Vantage Press, 1983.

Robson, J. *Christ in Islam*. London: John Murray, 1929.

Ryrie, Charles C. *Basic Theology*. Chicago, IL: Moody, 1981.

Schaff, Philip. *The Creeds of Christendom: with History and Critical Notes*, Edited by David S. Schaff, Vol. 1. *The History of the Creeds*. Grand Rapids, MI: Baker, 1983.

Shahid, Dr. Samuel. *The Fallen Nature of Man in Islam and Christianity*. Colorado Springs, CO: AL-Nour, 1989.

Smith, Chuck. *Answers for Today*. Costa Mesa, CA: The Word for Today, 1993.

Smith, John Pye. *The Scripture Testimony to the Messiah*. Edinburgh, Scotland: William Oliphant and Company, 1859.

Smith, Wilbur M. *Therefore Stand: Christian Apologetics*. Grand Rapids, MI: Baker, 1965.

Tisdall, William St. Clair. *Christian Reply to Muslim Objections*. Villach, Austria: Light of Life, 1904.

Walfson, Harry Austryn. *The Philosophy of the Kalam*. Cambridge, MA: Harvard Univ. Press, 1976.

Walvoord, John F. *Every Prophecy of the Bible*. Colorado Springs, CO: Cook Communications, 1999.

Wismer, D. *The Islamic Jesus*. New York: Gerland Publishing, Inc., 1977.

Zwemer, S. *The Moslem Christ*. London: Oliphant, Anderson and Ferrier, 1912.

———. *The Moslem Doctrine of God*. London: Oliphant, Anderson and Ferrier, 1905.

NOTES

As previously noted, all Islamic reference books listed below are recognized internationally in the Muslim world. They are republished annually and distributed in Muslim bookstores worldwide.

Introduction:

1. Ibn Hisham, *Al-Sira Al-Nabawiyya* (Beirut: Dar Al Kitab Al Arabi, 2013). Commentary by Dr. Omar Abd Al Salam Tadmory, Professor of Islamic History in Lebanon Universities. Muhammad saw his followers being persecuted by the ruling Quraysh tribe of Mecca, he sent his followers to migrate to the country of the Christian ruler, Negus of Abyssinia.

   The news that the Muslims were living in peace in Abyssinia reached Mecca. The leaders of the Quraysh tribe became angry, so they decided to send emissaries with presents of Mecca for Negus and his nobles and chiefs, to get the Muslims back from Abyssinia.

   Negus sent Quraysh agents back and refused their gifts.

   Negus treated the Muslims with honor and pledged his protection to them (Ibn Hisham, pp. 334–38). Ibn Hisham edited the biography of the Islamic prophet Muhammad written by Ibn Ishaq. It is now considered one of the classic works on the biography of the Islamic prophet Muhammad.

Chapter 1: Credibility of the Bible

1. The *Hadith* (Traditions) is the recorded sayings and actions of Muhammad, the prophet of Islam. This record is according to his wives, companions, members of his family, and Muslim leaders. The majority of the Muslim scholars of the world believe that the collections of the Hadith,

in Al-Bukhari and Muslim, are regarded as Holy Books in addition to the Qur'an. Therefore, the Hadith is the second source of Islamic religious authority after the Qur'an.

2. Colin Chapman, *You Go and Do the Same: Studies in Relating to Muslims* (London: CMS, 1983), 53.
3. Al-Tabari, *Commentary on the Qur'an* (Tafsir), Vol. 4, 649.
4. Ibn Hisham, *Al-Sira Al-Nabawiyya*, 267.

Chapter 3: The Gospel Is God's Glad News

1. David Shenk and Badru Kateregga, *A Muslim and A Christian in Dialogue* (Scottdale, PA: Herald Press, 1997), 142.
2. See Bibliography (McDowell).
3. Norman Geisler and William Nix, *From God to Us: How We Got Our Bible*, 139.
4. See Bibliography (Bruce; Geisler and Nix).
5. Henry H. Halley, *Halley's Bible Handbook*, 1092–1101.
6. See Bibliography (Morris).
7. See Bibliography (Walvoord).
8. H. M. Harman, *Introduction to the Study of the Holy Scriptures*, 488.
9. Ibid., 465.
10. Ibid., 464–65.
11. Ibid., 463–64.
12. Ibid., 52.

Chapter 5: Adam in Islam

1. Abdullah Yusuf Ali, in his Footnote 47 explains that the power of will when used aright brings the man nearer to the Godlike nature. (Note that the translation of Abdullah Yusuf Ali has become by far the most popular translation of the Qur'an into English in the Muslim world.)
2. Kassis, *A Concordance of the Qur'an*, (Berkeley, CA: University of California Press, 1983), 483.
3. Pickthall, *The Meaning of the Glorious Qur'an*, 47.
4. Abdullah Yusuf Ali, *The Meaning of the Holy Qur'an*, Note 53.
5. Kassis, *A Concordance of the Qur'an*, 595.
6. Note the *Hadith* is known as the Muslim *Traditions* and is a narration of what Muhammad said or did. It is considered an expression of divine revelation. It is accepted as a chief source of Islamic belief and practice and is second in authority only to the Qur'an.
   • *Sahih Al-Bukhari*, Vol. 8, Hadith No. 611 (according to Khan's Translation and ALIM's Translation).
   • Ibid., Vol. 9, Hadith No. 423 (ALIM's Translation and Khan's Translation).
   • Ibid., 4:552.

Chapter 6: The Results of the Fall

1. Chuck Smith, *Answers for Today*, 128.
2. *Sahih Al-Bukhari*, Vol. 8, Hadith No. 238 (ALIM's Translation and Khan's Translation).
3. *Sunan Ibn Majah*, Vol 5, 489.

Chapter 8: The Life of Abraham

1. Al-Tabari, *Commentary on the Qur'an*, Notes 29466–29468.
2. *Shorter Encyclopedia of Islam*, 175.
3. Abdullah Yusuf Ali, *The Holy Qur'an*, 1149, Note 4096.
4. Ibn Sa'd, *Kitab-al-Tabaqat al-Kabir*, Vol.1, 41.

Chapter 10: God Ransomed Abraham's Son

1. "Redeem" is defined in the dictionary: to free or rescue by paying a price or to free from the consequences of sin.
2. Dean C. Halverson, *The Compact Guide to World Religions*.
3. The word "ransom" means to "buy back." It is the payment demanded for the freedom of a captive.
4. *Sahih Al-Bukhari*, Vol. 2, Hadith No. 51 (Khan's Translation).
5. Al-Qasemi, *Commentary of the Holy Qur'an* (at Surah 3:45).

Chapter 11: Christ Jesus (AL-Masih, Isa) God's Anointed Mahasen al-Ta'aweel

1. See Bibliography (Lockyer).
2. Al-Baidawi commenting on Qur'an Surah 2:253.

Chapter 12: Jesus Christ, "His Word" (*Kalimatuhuu*)

1. Al-Razi, commenting on Surah 3:39.
2. Yousef al-Qaradawi and others, *t-Twahid*, 98.
3. Al-Baidawi, commenting on Qur'an Surah 3:39.
4. Harry Austryn Walfson, *The Philosophy of the Kalam*, (Cambridge: Harvard University Press, 1976), p. 251; quoted from Fisal Volume II, 5–6; and Vol. III, 5.
5. Ibid., 240–41 quoted from Al-Tabari, *Annals*, 118, Volume II, 10–11.

Chapter 13: Jesus Christ, "A Spirit from God" (*Ruhun Minhu*)

1. Al-Ahadith Al-Qudsiyyah, *Divine Narratives*, Hadith 112, 156–57.
2. Ibid., italics added.
3. Abdullah Yusuf Ali, *The Meaning of the Holy Qur'an*, Note 5365, italics added.

Chapter 14: The Virgin Birth of Jesus Christ

1. *Sahih Al-Bukhari* 6:71 (ALIM's Translation and Khan's Translation).

Chapter 15: The Sinlessness of Jesus Christ

1. *Sahih Al-Bukhari*, 4:506 (ALIM's Translation and Khans' Translation).
2. Ibid., Vol. 8, Hadith No. 89 (Khan's Translation).
3. Ibid., 4:501 (ALIM's Translation and Khan's Translation).
4. Ibid., 8:319 (ALIM's Translation and Khan's Translation).
5. Ibid., 8:379 (ALIM's Translation and Khan's Translation).
6. Ibid., 5:715: "O Allah! Forgive me, and bestow your mercy on me" (ALIM's Translation and Khan's Translation).
7. Ayoub Mahmoud M., *Towards an Islamic Christology II*, The Muslim World, Vol. LXX, No. 2, April 1980, 93.
8. Al-Baidawi, commenting on Qur'an Surah 5:110, italics added.

Chapter 16: Other Unique Features of Jesus' Life

1. Shukani, *Fath al- Qadir*.
2. Al-Razi, *Al-Tafsir Al-Kabir*.

Chapter 17: The Problem of Sin

1. *Sahih Al-Bukhari*, 4:501 (ALIM's Translation and Khan's Translation).
2. *Sunan Ibn-I-Majah*, Vol. 5, No. 4251.
3. "Islamic Government Does Not Spend for Its Own Grandeur," *Kayhan International* (September 4, 1985), 3.
4. Ibid.
5. *Al-Itqan*.
6. Sahih Al-Bukhari, Vol.5, Tradition No. 266 (Khan's Translation).
7. Ibid., Vol. 8, Tradition No. 470 (Khan's Translation).
8. Ibid., Vol.7, Tradition No. 577 (Khan's Translation).
9. Farid Esack, *On Being a Muslim* (Oxford: One World, 1999), 5.

Chapter 18: God Himself Came to Us in the Person of Jesus, the Messiah

1. Z. Assfy, *Islam and Christianity*, 6.
2. Badru Kateregga and David Shenk, *Islam and Christianity*, 19.
3. Ibid., 97–98.
4. *Sahih Al-Bukhari*, Vol. 8, Hadith No. 246, 160.

Chapter 20: The Crucifixion of Christ According to Islam

1. G. Parrinder, *Jesus in the Qur'an*, 121.
2. Abdullah Yusuf Ali, *The Meaning of the Holy Qur'an*, Footnote 2469.
3. A. H. Obaray, *Miraculous Conception, Death, Resurrection and Ascension of Jesus as Taught in the Qur'an*, 45.
4. The Azhar University in Egypt has been regarded as the light of Islam for the entire Islamic world.
5. Mahmud Shaltut, *Quoted in the Muslim World*, xxxiv, 214f.
6. Abdullah Yusuf Ali, *The Meaning of the Holy Qur'an*, Footnote 663.
7. Ibid., Footnote 664.
8. Al-Razi, Vol. VI:12, 113.
9. Tafsir-Al Kabir Maududi, *The Meaning of the Qur'an*, 390.
10. Daryabadi, *The Holy Qur'an*, Volume 1, 96–A.

Chapter 21: The Crucifixion and Resurrection of Jesus According to the Gospel

1. Abaas Mahmood Al Akad, *The Genius of Christ, Dar Al Halal*.
2. Josh McDowell, *The New Evidence that Demands a Verdict*, 216–17.
3. See Bibliography (Smith, Wilbur), 425–26.

Chapter 23: The Second Coming of Jesus

1. Abdullah Yusuf Ali, *The Meaning of the Holy Qur'an*, Footnote 4662.
2. Nuzul Esa Alam, *Descencion of Jesus Christ*, 37.
3. *Sahih Al-Bukhari*, Vol. 4, Hadith No. 657, also Vol. 3, No. 425 (ALIM's Translation and Khan's Translation).

4. *Sahih Muslim*, English Translation, Hadith No. 7037.
5. *Sahih Al-Bukhari*, English-Arabic, 2:459.
6. Ibid., 9:243 (ALIM's Translation and Khan's Translation).
7. *Sahih Muslim*, Hadith No. 6924 (ALIM).
8. Ibid., Hadith No. 7015 (ALIM).
9. Ibid., Hadith No. 7000.

Chapter 25: Do Christians Worship Three Gods?

1. Al-Qartaby, commenting on Qur'an Surah 4:171.

Chapter 26: Understanding the Tri-unity (Trinity) of God

1. Dean C. Halverson, *The Compact Guide to World Religions*.
2. Al-Ghazzali, *Ihya' Ulumed-Din*, 4:263.
3. Shaarani, *Book of Yawakeet*.
4. Imam Abi Hanifah, *Al-Fiqh al-Akbar*, 33.
5. G. Parrinder, *Jesus in the Qur'an*.
6. Philip Schaff, *The Creeds of Christendom: with a History and Critical Notes*.

Chapter 27: Jesus Is the Eternal Son of God in a Unique Spiritual Sense

1 A. Kenneth Cragg, *The Call of the Minaret*, 290.

Chapter 28: Jesus Received Worship

1. Ibn Ishaq was an early Islamic Scholar. He left behind two comprehensive works on the life of Muhammad. His work is still considered today an essential source for everyone who wants to learn about Muhammad's life and his companions.
2. A. Guillaume, *Life of Muhammad*, a translation of Ibn Ishaq's *Sirat Arasul*, 657.
3. Al-Razi, *Al-Tafsir Al-Kabir*, commenting on Surah 3:39, 211.
4. Ibid.
5. Ibid.
6. Ibid.
7. Ibid., commenting on Surah 19:7.

Chapter 29: God Is Love

1. The kash-shaf of the *Al-Zamkhashri*, Vol. 3, 187. See also Al Jalalan.
2. Sheikh-Ul-Hadith Hafiz and Muhammed Kandhalwi, *Teachings of Islam*, Ch. 11, 41.
3. Refer to "The Successors of the Apostle," khalid Muhammad khalid, 93.
4. Al Jalalan.
5. Hafiz and Kandhalwi, *Teachings of Islam*, Ch. 7, 128.
6. Ibid. Umar, Ch. 11, 42.
7. Sahih Al-Bukhari, Vol.5, Tradition No. 266 (Khan's Translation).
8. Ibid., English-Arabic, 2:459.
9. Al-Ghazzali, Ninety-Nine Beautiful Names of God in Islam, 91.
10. Ibid.

ACKNOWLEDGMENTS

M y words cannot express my gratitude to my Living God for guiding and enabling me to serve Him through this book.

To my beloved wife, Hala, I pray that I will love you in the deepest way possible all the days of our lives. Thank you for loving me and supporting me since I met you. You are the best and most wonderful human being and friend I know.

I thank God always for my financial and prayer partners. God uses them so richly to enable me to communicate the message of God's love and salvation effectively to multitudes of people.

Thank you Moody Publishers for helping get this book into the hands of many readers.

My appreciation goes to Gabriel Straight for providing the technical support for this book.

I am forever grateful to my gracious editors Marilyn Tyner and John Dunham.

A WORD FROM MY HEART
TO ALL FOLLOWERS OF JESUS

I am inviting all true believers and followers of Jesus Christ to manifest God's love to our precious Muslim neighbors and intentionally unite together in the goal of helping Muslims experience God's love and salvation.

ABOUT THE AUTHOR

Samy Tanagho was born and raised in Egypt where he studied Islamic law, culture, and religion. He later practiced law as a defense attorney and now lives in America.

Because Samy mastered the Arabic language, he was able to read the words of Muhammad and his companions and followers, which were written only in Arabic. He was able to read the books of the most important Muslim scholars and commentators, who interpreted the words of Muhammad and the Qur'an.

Samy serves as founder and president of the Glad News for Muslims non-profit corporation. Samy has been sharing Jesus with Muslims for over 30 years. His passion is to teach Christians to effectively communicate God's love and salvation to all people, including Muslims. He speaks on this topic throughout the United States and overseas. His wife, Hala, often joins him to share her story of imprisonment in Egypt for converting from Islam to Christianity.

Samy is also the author of *The True Love*. He ministers to Muslims through satellite TV, and he has a radio program, broadcast in many states, to motivate and equip Christians to share Jesus effectively with Muslims.

For more resources,
including witnessing tools
and Samy's video messages,
please visit
gladnewsministry.com